THE BATTLE OF THE
HUERTGEN FOREST

THE BATTLE OF THE HUERTGEN FOREST

CHARLES B. MacDONALD

UNIVERSITY OF PENNSYLVANIA PRESS

Philadelphia

Originally published 1963 by J.B. Lippincott Company
Copyright © 1963 Charles B. MacDonald

Printed in the United States of America on acid-free paper

10 9 8 7 6 5 4 3

Published 2003 by
University of Pennsylvania Press
Philadelphia, Pennsylvania 19104-4011

Library of Congress Cataloging-in-Publication Data

MacDonald, Charles Brown, 1922–
    The Battle of the Huertgen Forest / Charles B. MacDonald
        p. cm.
    ISBN 0-8122-1831-0 (pbk : alk. paper)
    First published Philadelphia, Lippincott [1963]
    Includes bibliographical references and index
        1. United States. Army—History—World War, 1939–1945. 2. Hürtgen,
Battle of, 1944. I. Title
D756.5.H8 M3   2002
940.54'213551—dc21   2002026609

The maps in this volume were drawn by B. C. Mossman.

For

Joy, Moire, Bruce

and

the men who were there

CONTENTS

viii] CONTENTS

MAPS

THE BATTLE OF THE HUERTGEN FOREST

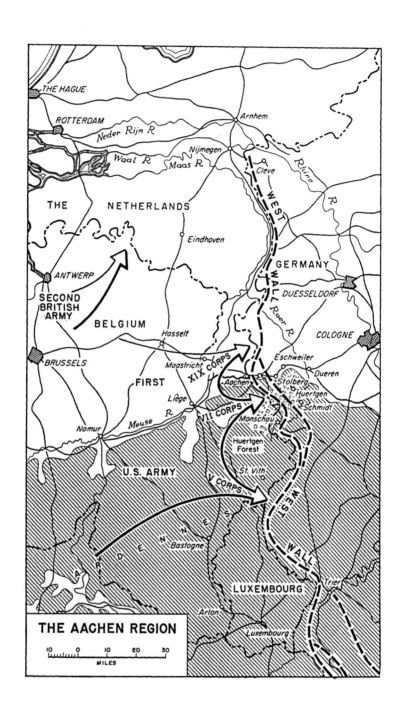

THE HAGUE

ROTTERDAM

Neder Rijn R.

Waal R.   Maas R.   Nijmegen

Arnhem

Cleve

Rhine R.

THE   NETHERLANDS

WEST

Eindhoven

GERMANY

ANTWERP

DUESSELDORF

SECOND
BRITISH
ARMY

BELGIUM

WALL

Roer R.

COLOGNE

Hasselt

BRUSSELS

Maastricht

XIX CORPS

Eschweiler

Dueren

FIRST

Aachen   Stolberg   Huertgen
Schmidt

Liège

VII CORPS

Meuse R.

Monschau

Namur

Huertgen
Forest

U.S. ARMY

St. Vith

V CORPS

WEST

A R D E N N E S

Bastogne

WALL

LUXEMBOURG   Trier

Arlon

Luxembourg

THE AACHEN REGION

10   0   10   20   30
MILES

A FOREST OUT OF
OLD FOLK TALES

1   HUERTGEN WAS THE NAME that caught on.

This is strange in a way, for the small plot of woodland the mapmakers label "Huertgen Forest" is but part of a great forest mass, twenty miles long and ten miles wide. In the three wet, cold, incredibly miserable months from mid-September to mid-December 1944, the fighting covered almost every inch of the entire forest mass. But Huertgen was the name that caught on.

Perhaps the American soldier used the name Huertgen because of the village of Huertgen. Guarding access to one of the high, bald ridges that rise near the eastern edge of the forest, this village was for so long a specified but unrealized objective of the campaign, a symbol of the frustration, even desperation, that characterized the fighting. Or perhaps to the soldier Huertgen sounded like "hurt" with a German ending.

Yet to accept either or both these explanations is to ignore the fact that to the German soldier, too, the entire forest mass came to have but one name: *Huertgenwald.*

The fact is, the Huertgen Forest to the American, *Huertgenwald* to the German, ceased to have any real geographical meaning. It was a forest, but it was more than a forest.

It was a special, grim way of fighting a war.

It was a special, grim way of dying.

Passchendaele with tree bursts, Ernest Hemingway called it.

The forest—what is left of it—stands along the Belgian–German border near Aachen, or Aix-la-Chapelle. It is at once the northernmost tip of both the Ardennes region of Belgium and Luxembourg and the Eifel region of Germany. Together the Ardennes–Eifel is one high plateau of ancient volcanic origin, divided only by the artificial international frontiers. To the eye of anyone but a geologist, the region appears to be less plateau than mountains, but this is primarily because through the centuries irascible streams have gouged the surface of the plateau with deep, serpentine cuts.

For hundreds of years the Ardennes–Eifel has stood like a big stone around which eddied traffic in peace and war. To the south is France. To the north is the relatively open country that may be called the Aachen Gap. Until modern times military forces had moved north or south of the big stone. But in 1914 the Imperial German Armies spilled over from the Aachen Gap into the Ardennes, and in 1940 Adolf Hitler opened his World War II campaign in the West with a surprise blow through the Ardennes that led to Dunkirk and the fall of France.

Nowhere in the Ardennes–Eifel are the draws and valleys deeper, the slopes more precipitous, than in the region the American soldier called the Huertgen Forest. It is as if the land had indulged in a final, frenzied convolution before grudgingly giving way to gently undulating plains stretching to the Rhine River around Cologne. The most pronounced of all the cuts is the gorge of the Roer River, rising near the picturesque border town of Monschau, sixteen miles south of Aachen. The Roer forms the southern and eastern boundaries of the forest, while the frontier generally traces the western limits. The northern reaches are jagged and ill defined, conforming to the last heaves before the land falls abruptly to the plain leading to the Rhine.

The source of the Roer and countless lesser streams that

slice the Huertgen Forest into a labyrinth of gloomy glens, the source also of the medicinal waters that have made the city of Aachen a popular watering place since Roman times, is a great stretch of high marshland or moor called the "Hohe Venn." Though most of the moor lies in Belgium, it extends across the border into the Huertgen Forest. Thus much of the soil in the forest, even that atop many of the hills and ridges, is a sponge.

In September 1944, when Allied armies under General Dwight D. Eisenhower neared the German border from the North Sea to Switzerland, it would have been difficult to convince anyone that the Huertgen Forest presented any genuine danger or hardship. Already the Germans had fled from the great forests of the Ardennes. What reason was there to believe they would not do the same from the Huertgen?

Entering the Huertgen Forest, thick with dark-green fir trees seventy-five to a hundred feet tall, so densely interwoven that they obscure the sky, a man might experience for the first time the stifling embrace of the kind of forests he had heard or read about in old German folk tales. Like Hansel and Gretel, he might be inclined to drop things behind him to mark his path. But it was hardly likely, in September 1944, that trouble lurked in the forest. For the Germans—it was obvious to all but the Germans—were beaten. It was only a question of time before the war would be over.

Having become established in Europe by means of spectacular amphibious landings in Normandy and southern France, British, French, Canadian, and American armies had chased defeated German forces across France and Belgium with a speed almost unknown in warfare. The question was no longer who would win the war but how the Allies might wrap up the victory.

Bowing to persistent requests of the senior British commander, Field Marshal Sir Bernard L. Montgomery, General Eisenhower had strengthened the British and Canadian armies of Montgomery's 21st Army Group by sending the First U.S. Army close alongside Montgomery's forces through Belgium. This was primarily to assure early capture of the Channel ports, including the great Belgian port of Antwerp, but it resulted in the First Army's entering Germany by way of the Ardennes and the Aachen Gap rather than south of the Ardennes, as had earlier been the plan.

This meant that the barrier of the Ardennes–Eifel would split Lt. Gen. Omar N. Bradley's 12th Army Group, composed of the First and Third U.S. Armies. The First Army's presence at Aachen meant also that Montgomery's armies would attempt the invasion of Germany not through the Aachen Gap but across the canal-creased lowlands of The Netherlands.

Yet in September 1944 neither of these apparent divergencies from standard military practice appeared to matter much. The Germans might elect to hold at their western border for reasons of prestige and to exact some benefit from the West Wall, or Siegfried Line, a series of fortifications along the border; but early withdrawal behind the historic moat of the Rhine was inevitable. This was the almost unanimous view of Allied intelligence officers. Furthermore, General Eisenhower's plan for the invasion of Germany contemplated no single thrust deep into the enemy country but instead a general build-up along the Rhine, followed by a "broad front" advance all along the line.

The First Army approached the German border with three corps abreast. On the south, the V Corps moved directly through the Ardennes. The VII Corps in the center approached the Huertgen Forest and the southern portion of the Aachen Gap. The XIX Corps, two days' march behind the others because of a gasoline shortage that had portentous overtones, headed for the open country north of Aachen.

The First Army—and the corps, divisions, and separate units serving under it—consisted of a force of some 250,000 men that had come ashore on D day in Normandy, made the big break from the beachhead, and liberated Paris. The commander was a fifty-seven-year-old veteran of World War I, Lt. Gen. Courtney H. Hodges. Though the First Army might appear colorless when compared to the Third Army, this was not a result of any legitimate disparity of accomplishments but rather of the affinity between the press and the Third Army commander, Lt. Gen. George S. Patton, Jr. While

Hodges appreciated what publicity could do for the morale of his troops, he himself lacked the personal color, eccentricity, or flamboyance to make good copy.

Of medium height and build, moustache closely trimmed, Courtney Hodges looked less the battlefield commander than the established businessman, and like a businessman he ran his army. He lacked the distinctive appearance of a Bradley, the studied flair of a Patton, the outspokenness of a Mark Clark, the dramatic bent of a Douglas MacArthur. Calm, sometimes aloof, Hodges eschewed profanity and rarely let his temper show. On the other hand, he could be quietly firm, almost ruthless, in dealing with a subordinate whose performance he questioned. Equally painstaking in planning and supervision, he seemed to some critics unduly cautious.

Like the U.S. Army's Chief of Staff, General George C. Marshall, who in 1941 gave Hodges' career a boost when he brought him to Washington as Chief of Infantry, Hodges was not a product of West Point. He flunked out of the military academy in his plebe year, then enlisted and gained a commission from the ranks. During World War I he earned the Distinguished Service Cross in the Meuse–Argonne Campaign. In early 1944 he left for England to become deputy commander of the First Army under Bradley, his eventual rise to command of the army once Bradley moved up to army group a foregone conclusion. This happened in August, slightly more than a month before Hodges and the First Army reached the German border.

Hodges' First Army in September contained eight veteran combat divisions and three mechanized cavalry groups. These were apportioned to the three corps in equal allotments of two infantry divisions, an armored division, and a cavalry group, except that the XIX Corps was temporarily short an infantry division. Also part of the army outside divisional organization were nine separate tank battalions, twelve tank-destroyer battalions, forty-six field-artillery battalions, and numbers of other highly specialized engineer, signal, anti-aircraft, chemical, quartermaster, transportation, ordnance, and medical units that went to make up a modern, mobile army at this stage of World War II.

Strong in infantry officers, the First Army staff reflected the infantry background of Hodges' predecessor, Omar Bradley, and of Hodges himself. Mindful that the First Army was the patriarch of U.S. armies in Europe, the staff was proud, stubborn, demanding. The First Army, everybody up to Eisenhower acknowledged, was a prima donna.

Though Hodges depended strongly on the counsel of his staff, there were many who would say that the one man who really had Hodges' ear was the commander whose troops were approaching the Huertgen Forest and part of the Aachen Gap. This was Maj. Gen. J. Lawton Collins of the VII Corps. Young at forty-eight, handsome, ebullient, Joe Collins was the very image of the all-American boy. Despite his youthful appearance, Collins, too, had fought in France in the Great War, and already during World War II had earned a reputation for dynamism and drive, and the nickname "Lightning Joe."

So often were the divisions assigned to Collins' VII Corps the most experienced available in the First Army that many believed that Joe Collins was Courtney Hodges' fair-haired boy. In September 1944, for example, Collins had the 1st and 9th Infantry Divisions, both of which had been fighting since the North African Campaign of 1942. He also had the "heavy" 3d Armored Division, one of three such divisions organized before the U.S. Army scaled down the tank strength of its armored divisions from 232 to 168.

The First Army's other two corps commanders were quite unlike Collins. One, Charles H. Corlett of the XIX Corps, was a sick man doing his utmost to keep up the pace, whose physical condition precluded his staying much longer at the front. The other was Leonard T. Gerow of the V Corps, who was in many ways like Courtney Hodges. Almost the same age as Hodges, taciturn, steady, a meticulous planner with long experience in top echelons of the War Department, Gerow supervised his divisions closely, almost dictatorially, particularly in planning phases. Average in height and build, Gerow had only one distinctive physical feature that set him apart. This was his eyes, which were set in coal-like sockets that made them seem penetrating and profound.

As was often the case with the First Army, it was Joe

Collins who set the pace of the thrust across the German border. While the first patrols penetrated the frontier late on September 11, General Hodges believed—with considerable reason—that at least a two-day pause was imperative. His corps and divisions were advancing in spread formation along a front of more than 120 miles. The XIX Corps on the left still had some twenty miles to go before catching up with the rest of the army. Furthermore, the great pursuit had made serious inroads on the army's equipment. Of 1,010 authorized medium tanks, for example, only 850 actually were on hand, many of these so badly in need of maintenance that they could not fight a sustained engagement. Of 232 tanks authorized for the 3d Armored Division, only 75 were in condition to fight. Whereas gasoline and transportation for the infantry had held high priority during the pursuit, the fortifications along the German border made it likely that artillery would now be the main item. Many of the big guns had been left far behind, their prime movers commandeered to lift the infantry. Ammunition, too, had been low on the priority lists during the pursuit. Though the First Army received a thousand tons of ammunition on September 11, not until four days later would enough be on hand at the front for five days of intensive fighting.

Loath to upset the impetus of victorious troops, Hodges ordered a two-day halt. Bridge the period, he said, with extensive reconnaissance.

Chafing at even two days' delay, Collins protested. Don't stop men when they're moving, Collins insisted. He wanted to mount a "reconnaissance in force" early the next day, September 12, in order to breach the border fortifications of the Siegfried Line before the Germans had a chance to man them.

Why not get past the fortifications first, then pause for supplies?

Hodges backed down. Go ahead, he told both Collins and Leonard Gerow of the V Corps. But if they ran into "solid" opposition, he added, and failed to achieve "quick" penetrations, they were to halt to await supplies. Only after they had stocked up on artillery and ammunition were they to launch full-scale attacks.

STIRRINGS IN THE
GERMAN CAMP

2 THROUGHOUT THE NIGHT of September 11, confusion, anxiety, and gloom paraded ostentatiously around the headquarters of the German *Seventh Army*,* hastily set up in a brick barracks near a little town twenty-three miles inside the Eifel. Hardly had night fallen when the bad news reached the army commander. The disaster everybody had been predicting for days, General der Panzertruppen Erich Brandenberger learned, had come to pass. The *2d Panzer Division*, withdrawing hurriedly from Belgium and Luxembourg to occupy the pillboxes and bunkers of the West Wall, had found the Americans already there.

Even though the dawn brought news that the reports were false, that only patrols had entered the West Wall and then withdrawn, the atmosphere around Brandenberger's headquarters failed to brighten appreciably. Even if the Americans had not come yesterday, they would arrive today, tomorrow, or the day after. Whenever they came, the *Seventh Army* simply had not the men, machines, weapons, or ammunition to stop them.

There was only one genuinely encouraging aspect in the whole situation of the *Seventh Army:* despite the haste of the

* To simplify identification references to bodies of German troops are printed in italics.

flight from France, corps and division headquarters had remained basically intact. Thus a framework to hang reinforcements on existed—*if* reinforcements could be found in time.

On the south wing of the army, opposite Luxembourg, was the *1st SS Panzer Corps,* with remnants of two panzer divisions. In the center, in the forests on either side of Monschau, was the *74th Corps.* Commanded by General der Infanterie Erich Straube, this corps controlled remnants of two infantry divisions. In the north, beyond Monschau, covering part of the forest and all the Aachen Gap, was the *81st Corps* under Generalleutnant Friedrich-August Schack. This corps had four badly mauled divisions, two of them infantry, the other two the once-proud *9th* and *116th Panzer Divisions.*

Relatively stable organization also still existed at higher echelons. Indeed, the German order of battle on the Western Front looked in early September much as it had before Allied troops landed in Normandy.

Controlling the northern half of the front, opposite the British along the Dutch–Belgian border and the First U.S. Army, was *Army Group B.* The commander was Generalfeldmarschall Walter Model, a devoted disciple of Adolf Hitler, the German *Fuehrer.* A newcomer to the Western Front, Model had spent the earlier years of the war in Russia building a reputation as a master of improvised defense. One of the first to reaffirm allegiance after a clique of officers in July had tried to kill the *Fuehrer,* Model was a man whom Hitler could trust. Arriving in mid-August, he had become both the Commander in Chief in the West and head of *Army Group B,* an interim-command arrangement, which would stand until Hitler got around to naming another commander for one post or the other.

A man who spoke his mind, even to his *Fuehrer,* Model made no effort to conceal the extent of the defeat in France. Appraised of the facts, Hitler decided he had no alternative but to turn again to a man he earlier had removed as Commander in Chief—the venerable old soldier, that paragon of all that was good and right with the German Officer Corps, Gerd von Rundstedt. Hitler saw Rundstedt as a symbol around which the faltering troops might rally. While installing Rundstedt in the top post, he left the trusted Model to contrive a steadfast defense along the invasion route Allied armies were most likely to choose, the route north of the Ardennes–Eifel. To carry out the task, Model had three armies, including Brandenberger's *Seventh*.

The other half of the front was the responsibility of *Army Group G*, composed of two armies, one confronting the Third U.S. Army in Lorraine, the other facing the 6th Army Group (Seventh U.S. and First French Armies), mainly in Alsace. A third, the *Fifth Panzer Army*, was assembling behind the German border.

Thus all major German units which had fought earlier in the West were present and accounted for—in name, at least—and their commanders and staffs were still basically intact at all levels above regiment. That this could be the case after a defeat in the field of such proportions was attributable to the German penchant for organization and discipline, obviously the only real hope at this stage for recovery in the West and thus for salvaging anything from the war Hitler had started with the invasion of Poland in 1939.

All of Germany itself, including East Prussia, was, of course, still inviolate. Some of the earlier conquests—Denmark, Norway, The Netherlands, Czechoslovakia, Austria, Yugoslavia, Albania, and Greece—were also intact, as were three allies, Finland, Hungary, and Bulgaria. But the massive Red tide from the East, swelling full-blooded and apparently irrepressible from the wellspring of Stalingrad, already by early September 1944 had driven Nazi forces from Soviet Russia, reconquered much of the three Baltic states, and overrun more than half of Poland and Romania. The erstwhile major ally, Benito Mussolini's Fascist Italy, had long since chosen the ignominious path of surrender. German troops still held the northern half of Italy, but armies of the Western Allies had swept the Italian boot to a line well north of Rome.

It had been a long, hard five years of war. Already the German armed forces had lost over 3,700,000 men killed, captured, or permanently disabled. A lion's share of these had been army losses. With intense fighting on three major fronts —the East, Italy, and France—the summer months of 1944 had been the worst of all, bringing losses in killed, wounded, and missing of more than 1,200,000. Losses in weapons and equipment—aircraft, tanks, artillery, transport—had been so enormous as to defy estimate.

Ringed on three sides by powerful adversaries only just reaching the peak of their fighting potential, a man more rational than Adolf Hitler might have been inclined to take the advice one of his earlier Commanders in Chief in the West had proffered in a suicide note—make peace. But to Hitler, this advice meant only one thing: too many in the hierarchy of the old German Officer Corps were not to be trusted. It was this lack of confidence, fed by continuing defeats in the East, that had prompted Hitler to take conduct of the war more and more into his own hands. The July attempt on Hitler's life had convinced the *Fuehrer* beyond a doubt that he was right to distrust his officers. From this point, Hitler himself, a man far removed from the practical considerations of the battlefield and untrained in military methodology, had taken personal charge of the war. For the Western Front this had spelled a strategy that could be summed up in two words: "Stand Fast." No commander, Hitler decreed, could undertake any withdrawal without express permission of the *Fuehrer*.

The fact was that from Hitler's Jovian position, all was not the gloom and doom it appeared at lower levels. As of September 1944, for example, the German armed forces (*Wehrmacht*) still contained some 10,100,000 men, more than 7,500,000 of whom were in the army and a specialized army auxiliary, the *Waffen-SS*. That many of these men were of poor quality and that the bulk of the army was on the man-eating Eastern Front went without saying. On the other hand, the disparity between Allied and German forces on the Western Front was not irreparable. While the Allied commander, General Eisenhower, had forty-nine divisions, the Germans, theoretically, at least, had forty-eight infantry and fifteen panzer divisions, plus several panzer brigades. Though these forces might be equal numerically to only about half those of the Allies, the command apparatus for absorbing replacements and new subordinate units was intact.

It was in air forces and equipment, particularly tanks and artillery, that the Germans were most inferior. Allied superiority in guns was at least 2½ to 1; in tanks, approximately 20 to 1; and in aircraft, overwhelming. The Allies had four tactical air forces in the West to one weak German force. There were 13,891 American and British planes active in the skies over the West, almost half of them fighters. To oppose these and the Russians' aircraft, the entire German *Luftwaffe* had only 4,507 serviceable planes.

To the German grenadier, scurrying homeward past carcasses of tanks, trucks, half-tracked personnel carriers, horses, wagons, always under the eyes of the *jabos* (as he called Allied fighter planes), there might appear to be no possible solution. But, in reality, the genius of German production still was on his side. Despite round-the-clock bombings of unprecedented magnitude, the Germans had been able to maintain an incredibly high rate of production. In September, for example, some twenty-five new submarines, most of which were equipped with the Schnorkel underwater "breathing" device, would be launched. Also in September, German factories would begin to redress the balance in aircraft, and new jet-propelled planes promised for early delivery soon might offset any remaining imbalance.

In regard to tanks, Hitler as early as June had acted to narrow the gap between German and Allied armored strength by concentrating on models tactically superior to the Allied mainstay, the American Sherman tank. In August, in addition to the 279 medium tanks that came off the assembly line, 455 heavy tanks were also built.

Priority on the new, more powerful tanks went to the West, where ten new panzer brigades were being equipped, each built around a tank battalion. Creation of these brigades was one of several steps that Hitler had begun to take to bolster manpower as well as build up equipment in the West. During the summer he had already raised fifteen new divisions by returning troops to duty from hospitals, extending both ends of the induction spectrum, converting sailors and airmen into infantrymen, and otherwise combing out rear areas. Most of these divisions had gone to the East, but now, as the full extent of the defeat in France became apparent, Hitler ordered formation of twenty-five more divisions, almost all destined for the West between the end of September and the first of December. With a salaam to the national pride of the German people (*das Volk*), these were called *volksgrenadier* divisions. They contained about 10,000 men, some 2,500 fewer than the standard German infantry division of the time. For manpower the divisions were to substitute firepower. Two platoons in each company were to be armed with a rapid-firing machine pistol, and the division was to contain fourteen assault guns (self-propelled close-support weapons) and slightly higher than normal complements of artillery and antitank weapons.

Hitler took still another drastic step to bolster the West. Some hundred so-called "fortress infantry battalions," heretofore used only in rear areas, were hastily re-equipped and hurried to the front. Though many men in these units were overage, undertrained, or politically unreliable, they still would give a good enough account of themselves to prompt the First U.S. Army to refer to them later as the "hidden reserve" in large measure responsible for the outcome of the early fighting on the German frontier.

More than any of his field commanders, Hitler put immense faith in the frontier fortifications, the West Wall. Construction of a West Wall had first begun in 1938, after Hitler had sent troops into a Rhineland demilitarized under terms of the Versailles Treaty. Originally designed as a short belt of fortifications opposite the French Maginot Line, it had been extended from the Swiss border to a point well north of Aachen. Unlike the Maginot Line, it was no thin band of elaborate forts but a belt, averaging three miles in depth, of hundreds of mutually supporting pillboxes, observation and command posts, troop shelters, and bunkers.

The two strongest portions of the line opposed the Maginot Line and barred the Aachen Gap. The latter was actually two lines, one close along the frontier called the Scharnhorst Line, the other five miles to the rear called the Schill Line. The first of the two was the thinner, but gained added strength from a continuous band of antitank obstacles in front of it. These were pyramid-shaped concrete projections called "dragon's teeth," disposed across the hills and valleys like some endless, scaly-backed reptile. Pillboxes in both lines were thickest across the relatively open ground around Aachen, though the same arrangement of two lines also existed in the great forested region around Monschau.

A typical pillbox was about 25 feet wide, 45 feet deep, and 20 feet high, with walls and roof of reinforced concrete from 3 to 8 feet thick. At least half the structure lay underground. Each pillbox contained web-bottomed bunks arranged in tiers to accommodate a usual complement of about fourteen men. Most had two firing embrasures. Though these embrasures provided only limited fields of fire, the pillboxes were arranged in clusters, so that guns in one could cover the approaches to several others.

The same belt of fortifications that to the Germans was the West Wall was to the Allied soldiers the Siegfried Line. Probably a throwback to World War I, when the Germans labeled one of their second lines of defense the *Siegfriedstellung*, the name came into common use from a tune popular in British music halls early in the war, "I'm Going to Hang My Washing on the Siegfried Line."

Irreverence toward the line was markedly impolitic at that stage of the war, for in the 1939–40 period many military analysts considered the line impregnable. A large part of this reputation obviously rested on propaganda, but in those days the West Wall clearly would have been a serious obstacle. Though never designed to stop an attack indefinitely, but merely to delay it until mobile reserves could arrive, the line in 1940 could have been bolstered with strength sufficient to eject the foe.

As the West Wall stood in September 1944, it was something of a Potemkin village. There existed no strong reserves to back up the line, and, indeed, there were not even enough men to occupy all positions. Nor could the pillboxes accommodate guns larger than the standard 37mm. antitank gun, which was effective against the armor of 1940 but little better than a peashooter in 1944. Some of the positions could not even accommodate the 1944 German machine gun.

To the German commander or soldier moving into these outdated, neglected West Wall pillboxes, hope of making a strong stand was slight. But Hitler did not agree. Not only would the West Wall provide added strength, he reasoned, but unfavorable campaigning weather and the inhospitable terrain along the frontier—particularly the forests and deep chasms of the Eifel—would further retard an Allied force that Hitler believed had already outrun its supply lines.

To German commanders on the scene, the question was whether the forces left to them were sufficient to take advantage of the frontier obstacles. Nowhere was there more doubt than in the *Seventh Army,* where bald, full-jowled, bespectacled Erich Brandenberger favored quick withdrawal behind the Rhine. Meticulous, almost scientific in the way he handled his army—much like his opposite on the Allied side, General Hodges—Brandenberger was not a man to be upset by crisis. Just the opposite: he appeared to bloom under adversity. But adversity and futility are two different things. No experienced professional could ignore the near chaos existing in Brandenberger's subordinate units and the dearth of reinforcements.

On the *Seventh Army's* south wing, defending the heart of the Eifel, the *1st SS Panzer Corps* could muster no more than 2,000 fighting men and—most shocking of all for a panzer corps—only six tanks. Yet General Straube's *74th Corps* in the center around Monschau was weaker still. Of Straube's two divisions, the one south of Monschau was so understrength that when a training regiment and a fortress battalion were attached, the newcomers exceeded the veterans 10 to 1. The other, the *89th Infantry Division* around Monschau, had only one regiment with but 350 men. Commanded by Col. Eberhard Roesler, this division long ago had used up its artillerymen, engineers, and service troops as infantry. Upon arrival at the West Wall, Roesler received enough local security and fortress troops to provide a nucleus for a second regiment, but these were culls nobody could get excited about. He received also seventy-five antitank guns of varying caliber. For artillery, Roesler had four Russian 122mm. howitzers, a German light howitzer, and an Italian medium howitzer. Since he had no ammunition for the Italian piece, Roesler told his men to tow it ostentatiously about the front, to make it look as if he had a lot of guns.

General Brandenberger's strongest corps was Schack's *81st Corps* astride the Aachen Gap. Of four seriously weakened divisions, the two defending the West Wall north of Aachen would gain a few days respite while the XIX U.S. Corps was coming forward. Of the other two, the *116th Panzer Division* was actually on hand, but the *9th Panzer Division* still was moving from an assembly area where Rundstedt, the new Commander in Chief in the West, had seized upon it as the only reserve available on the entire Western Front for use at Aachen.

Nominally, the *81st Corps* had two other units, but one, a panzer brigade, had lost most of its tanks in front of the West Wall early on September 11, and the other, the *353d Infantry Division*, had only a division headquarters. The *81st Corps* commander, General Schack, put the infantry headquarters in a back-up position in the second band of the West Wall, the Schill Line, in charge of a training regiment and a conglomeration of local security and fortress battalions. The panzer brigade he merged with early arrivals of the *9th Panzer Division*, numbering about 300 men. The early arrivals included two artillery batteries but no tanks.

It seemed to Schack that his best chance for preventing a breakthrough until help arrived would be to concentrate his greatest strength before what he considered to be the immediate American objective, the city of Aachen. Shoring up the *116th Panzer Division* with three fortress battalions, he entrusted defense of the city to the division commander, Generalleutnant Graf (Count) Gerhard von Schwerin. For blocking the presumably less-threatened sector between Aachen and the

Huertgen Forest, he depended on the incoming *9th Panzer Division.*

Hope that help might arrive in time to prevent an American breakthrough suddenly blossomed soon after daylight on the twelfth. From Hitler himself came word that he had earmarked two infantry divisions for early transfer to Field Marshal Model's *Army Group B.* Model promptly scheduled both for Brandenberger's *Seventh Army.*

This was all the encouragement Brandenberger needed. An indefatigable man who threw himself with fierce enthusiasm into his work, Brandenberger began to move like an impulsive machine: a fortress battalion shifted here, two fleeing antitank guns turned around and thrown in there; one exhortation after another to Schack and Straube to hold.

Advance contingents of the *12th Infantry Division,* Brandenberger told them, were to entrain in East Prussia at midnight, September 13, under priority orders from the *Fuehrer* himself. With any luck from the weather to screen the trains from Allied planes, first arrivals might show up in less than three days.

Unfortunately for the Germans, three days might be too late, for General Schack's opposite on the American side, Joe Collins of the VII Corps, had no intention of attacking where Schack anticipated. Undistracted by the glory of capturing Aachen, birthplace of the Emperor Charlemagne, capital of the Holy Roman Empire, site of the coronation of thirty-two emperors and kings, Collins saw the primary objective as the penetration of the Siegfried Line. And the place to do that was south of Aachen, between that city and the Huertgen Forest.

GERMAN VERSUS AMERICAN

3   PRODUCT OF A NATION whose industrial and manpower resources would never have to be totally mobilized to win World War II, the American soldier in the fall of 1944 was the best-paid and best-fed soldier in history. He was among the best clothed as well, though long experience on the bitter Eastern Front had taught his German adversary considerably more about winter clothing.

German and American arms were similar in quality, but the long war had severely reduced the quantity of German weapons. Though the basic shoulder weapon in the U.S. Army, a semiautomatic .30-caliber rifle, gave the American some firepower advantage over the German with his bolt-action 7.92mm. piece, widespread German use of an automatic machine-pistol similar to a submachine gun lessened the advantage. Because of a high cyclic rate of fire, the machine pistol had a distinctive emetic *B-r-r-r-r-r-r-p* sound, which prompted the nickname-prone Americans to call it a "burp gun." Within the U.S. rifle platoon, firepower to supplement the rifle came primarily from a World War I weapon, the .30-caliber Browning Automatic Rifle, called the B.A.R. Each squad had one of these.

The standard German machine gun was an air-cooled 1942 model, also with a high cyclic rate of fire. Its sound in firing contrasted sharply with the slow *Put-Put-Put* sound of the American machine gun, a carry-over from World War I. In both armies the machine gun was an integral part of the rifle company, though a heavier water-cooled version of the American piece was located in a special "heavy weapons" company within the rifle battalion.

In both German and American armies, the basic close-support mortar was an 81mm. piece. The American soldier also put considerable faith in little 60mm. mortars, of which each rifle company had three; but by the fall of 1944 the Germans had generally discarded a similar 50mm. piece as ineffective. The Germans had heavier mortars too and brought them increasingly into use late in 1944 to supplement their depleted artillery. The best known of these was the *Nebelwerfer*, a multiple-barrel 150mm. mortar mounted on wheels and fired electrically. Though the projectile of the *Nebelwerfer* made a terrifying sound that earned it the nickname "Screaming Meemie," the weapon was inaccurate and its shells had little fragmentation effect.

The two other most widely used weapons in the front lines were hand grenades and close-range antitank weapons. The Americans used a fragmentation grenade; the Germans a "potato masher" concussion grenade that had changed little since World War I. For close-in antitank defense, the Germans used a one-shot, shaped-charge piece called a *Panzerfaust;* and the Americans a rocket launcher called the bazooka.

The basic artillery pieces of both combatants were light and medium howitzers of similar caliber and performance. In both German and American infantry divisions, tables of organization called for one medium and three light artillery battalions, supplemented by additional units controlled by corps and army. Under normal conditions, one light battalion was assigned to direct support of each of the three infantry regiments in the division, while the medium battalion remained in general support of the entire division. Both German and American artillery in infantry divisions was, in theory, motor-towed, but the Germans increasingly had had to turn to horsepower. Self-propelled artillery was organic only to armored divisions.

Infantry divisions in both armies nevertheless had some self-propelled heavy-fire support. The Americans normally attached a tank battalion and a self-propelled tank-destroyer battalion to each infantry division, while self-propelled assault guns were organic to all German divisions. Though the tank destroyers and assault guns were comparable, the Americans tended to use their destroyers less for infantry assault support than as an antitank weapon or as a supplement to their artillery, leaving the support role to the tanks. The German assault gun was either a 75mm. or 88mm. high-velocity weapon; the American destroyer a 3-inch piece.

German tanks were in most ways superior to American tanks. Indeed, as many a tank crew protested and ordnance experts back in Washington consistently denied, the standard American tank, the Sherman, a 33-ton medium, was obsolescent. Mounting a short-barreled 75mm. gun, the Sherman was outgunned by the enemy's 63-ton Mark VI (Tiger) and the 50-ton Mark V (Panther), both mounting an 88mm. piece. The Tiger, the Panther, and even the medium Mark IV all had thicker armor than the Sherman. Though the Sherman possessed greater maneuverability on firm ground, German tanks had wider tracks for better flotation in soft soil. The American tank was easier to maintain, was more flexible, and could fire faster, but the only telling American superiority was in numbers.

If any German weapon can be said to have impressed the American soldier more than any other, it was the "88," a high-velocity 88mm. dual-purpose antiaircraft and antitank piece. Standard armament for the Panther and Tiger tanks, it was to be found also as an assault gun and sometimes as a towed weapon. Though numerous, the 88 was not nearly so ubiquitous as the American soldier believed; but it unquestionably was World War II's equivalent of the French 75.

It would be less simple to single out any one weapon on the American side that similarly impressed the German soldier, for the thing that struck the German most was the seemingly inexhaustible supply of American arms and ammunition. He nevertheless was particularly impressed with a fragile little

American airplane, the L-4. A seeming throwback to the days of the Wright brothers, the L-4 was invaluable for adjusting artillery fire and for spotting German artillery behind the lines. The Germans also paid considerable obeisance to the efficacy of American communications equipment and the way it made possible lightning calls and adjustment of artillery fire.

In organization, German and American divisions were roughly comparable, though the American infantry division with attachments numbered about 16,000 men and thus was stronger numerically than either the 12,500-man standard German division or the new 10,000-man *volksgrenadier*. All had three infantry regiments, though most German divisions had two instead of three battalions to the regiment. Armored or panzer divisions were also similar, each having three tank battalions and three battalions of mechanized infantry known either as "armored infantry" or "panzer grenadiers." (The three so-called "heavy" American armored divisions—like the 3d Armored—had instead one armored infantry and two tank regiments.) While the German battalions were organized into panzer and panzer grenadier regiments, the American equivalents maintained their identity as battalions while operating under a loose arrangement of three combat commands, CCA, CCB, and CCR (reserve). Both had additional reconnaissance forces and either tank destroyers or assault guns, plus artillery strength similar to that of the infantry divisions. The Americans had a third type of combat force, the cavalry group, in effect a mechanized light regiment, usually used for screening or long-range reconnaissance.

Tactics of the two opponents differed little except in the German dedication to counterattack. Seldom did the Germans give any ground without attempting to retake it almost immediately by counterattack, no matter how limited the resources at hand. The Americans were similarly dedicated to counterattack in principle, but they used it much more sparingly in practice.

The one really major difference between the two forces on the battlefield was the presence of American fighter aircraft. By September 1944 the *Luftwaffe* virtually had ceased to exist as a tactical force; during the course of the battle of the Huertgen Forest, for example, the *Luftwaffe* would make only one strike. The Americans, on the other hand, depended heavily on air support and could but bemoan the increasing number of days in the fall when unfavorable weather interfered with flights.

Each American field army had one tactical air command to support it. In the First Army, it was the Ninth Tactical Air Command under Maj. Gen. Elwood R. ("Pete") Quesada. Though the strength of the "Ninth TAC" varied, the headquarters usually controlled six fighter-bomber groups. A group normally had three squadrons of 25 planes each, either P-38's (Lightnings), P-47's (Thunderbolts), or P-51's (Mustangs). Requests for air support usually came from front-line divisions through an air section at corps headquarters; but since air targets could not always be anticipated, a fighter group often was assigned to a specific corps or division for an entire day to take advantage of lucrative targets as they appeared.

The one big drawback to successful American (and Allied) campaigning at this stage of the war was in the unglamorous but nonetheless vital field of logistics. Specifically, the trouble was overstrained supply lines and, thus, transportation. The Allies had plenty of gasoline, ammunition, and equipment on the Continent, but most of it was far back at the Normandy invasion beaches. In early September the only major port working for the Allies was Cherbourg, even farther from the front than the beaches. In the explosive August dash across France and Belgium, Allied armies had far outrun the logistics schedules that the slide-rule specialists had drawn up before the invasion. While expedients like the "Red Ball Express"—a one-way truck-supply route through France—might ease the logistical problem, supply shortages would continue to crimp operations until depots and other installations could be moved closer to the front and until a major port near the front could be opened. British capture of Antwerp on September 4 gave promise of a port, but the Germans were destined to cling like beggar-lice to the seaward approaches to Antwerp for many more weeks. In the end, the big Belgian port would not begin to work for the Allied cause until almost the end of November.

The logistical hangover—a direct result of the wild tactical revels of August—would prove a persistent headache.

PROLOGUE IN THE
SIEGFRIED LINE

4   TIDY, WELL-CONTAINED battles like Leuthen or Auster-
litz, Gettysburg or Sedan, went out of style with the coming
of World War I. The new concepts of tremendous masses of
men and long, continuous front lines saw to that. Now the very
meaning of the term *battle* was open to revision; for as both
the number of combatants and the battlefield area increased,
the climactic element that heretofore had characterized battles
was often missing. There might still be well-defined, short-
lived, decisive combats like the Battle of the Masurian Lakes
or the First Battle of the Marne, but there might also be
bloody, lengthy, inconclusive struggles like the First and Second Battles of the Somme and like Passchendaele. No matter
that they stretched over great periods of time and that a climax was missing. They qualified as battles nonetheless: series
of engagements fought for a common objective, occurring over
common terrain and under common battlefield conditions.

The battle of the Huertgen Forest was one of the latter.
There was nothing really decisive about it. The winning of
World War II was not dependent on who held this miserable
little stretch of woodland. Neither side brought all its available resources to bear, and through the grim three-month
struggle the cast of characters frequently changed. But what
took place in the forest was a "battle" nevertheless, distin-

guished from the rest of the fighting on the long front by the
objective, the terrain, the peculiar nature of the forest fighting
. . . and by the forest itself.

As the first American patrols neared the German frontier,
neither rank-and-file soldier nor high-echelon commander saw
the coming operations as anything more than a continuation of
the pursuit of beaten German armies. While the First Army
was pursuing the enemy through the Aachen Gap and the
wooded Eifel, British and Canadians with the help of a powerful Allied airborne army were to push through The Netherlands and leap the Lower Rhine. At the same time, the three
other Allied armies were to chase the defeated enemy from
Alsace and Lorraine.

It was only through a gradual process, a kind of slow evo-
lution, that the pursuit changed into a battle on the German
frontier, one that eventually broke down into a series of smaller
battles at various points. In the case of the First U.S. Army in
September 1944, the attempt by Gerow's V Corps to penetrate
the center of the Eifel quickly became a separate engagement,
while the efforts of Corlett's XIX Corps north of Aachen and
part of Collins' VII Corps south of the city to crack the Siegfried Line fused into a battle for Aachen. At the same time,
the woods and harsh terrain of the Huertgen Forest gradually,
almost imperceptibly, began to create a third engagement.

The battle of the Huertgen Forest thus began as an integral part of General Collins' reconnaissance in force to try to
get quickly through the Siegfried Line. Only after the forest
itself and German reaction there had had time to influence
the broader battle was the fighting in the forest to emerge as
a truly separate struggle.

Faced on one flank by Aachen and on the other by a dense
forest, Joe Collins planned from the start to make his main
effort between the two obstacles. Yet even this route posed
major disadvantages. Less than six miles wide at one point, the
land between woods and city rises and pitches like the course
of a roller coaster. It is cut by deep traces of three small rivers

and by big patches of timber which had been part of the Huertgen Forest until industrious hands cleared some of the trees and created farms, towns, and villages. Deposits of lignite (brown coal) spurred the growth of the small industrial city of Stolberg. Yet for all the obstructions, the route provided a semblance of a terrain corridor up which the main strength of the VII Corps might advance to pierce the fortifications and emerge on open ground leading to the Rhine. For convenience, but at the risk of creating an undue impression of its military utility, the route may be called the Stolberg Corridor.

Authorized to make no full-scale attack, only a reconnaissance in force, Collins assigned the task to the two combat commands of the 3d Armored Division, plus two battalions from the 1st Division. While the infantry reconnoitered toward Aachen, the armor was to strike directly up the Stolberg Corridor. If the Germans failed to fight back strongly, the 1st Division was to seize high ground overlooking Aachen, the armor was to push all the way through both bands of the Siegfried Line to the Roer River, some seventeen miles inside Germany, and the 9th Division was to sweep the Huertgen Forest.

In giving the main assignment to the 3d Armored Division, Collins put his hopes for a quick penetration in a man whom he considered the best division commander on the Allied side. This was Maj. Gen. Maurice Rose. A few years younger than Collins, Rose was a man from the ranks, tough, over six feet tall, with crew-cut hair and firm, almost belligerent jaw.

As the troops headed for the border on September 12, just why some of Joe Collins' drive and sense of urgency and Maurice Rose's determination and daring failed to rub off on the men under them was hard to say. To many a man the war was almost over—who wanted to be killed this late in the game? To many a man too there was something foreboding, even sinister, about the towns and the countryside as they neared the frontier. This was borderland, ceded to Belgium after World War I, where the natives stood sullen and inscrutable on the street corners, an abrupt, chilling change from the tumultuous welcome the men had come to know. It was a place where street names and shop signs were in German, often in the ponderous old German script that looked like kissing kin of swastikas. It was a place, too, where a strange smell of burning peat, a heavy, German smell, filled the air, where the trees were towering firs that shut out the light and scowled at any who walked below. And up ahead, perhaps around the next bend in the road, or in the next clearing, stood the pillboxes of the Siegfried Line, allegedly the most formidable fortifications in the world.

No matter what the reason, the reconnaissance in force on September 12 not only failed to penetrate the Siegfried Line; it almost failed to reach the line. After losing three tanks to a nest of cleverly camouflaged antitank guns, one of the armored combat commands stopped for the night just over half a mile short of the dragon's teeth. The other reached the line in mid-afternoon near the village of Roetgen, about halfway between Aachen and Monschau, but on one side of the road dragon's teeth barred passage, on the other was a precipice, and in the road itself was a big crater.

The Germans of Friedrich Schack's *81st Corps* thus gained another day in their scramble to get men to defend the pillboxes, yet few on the German side of the dragon's teeth could discern any real hope of holding until the promised new division arrived. The city of Aachen that night, for example, was Moscow with Napoleon on the march after Borodino. A non-Nazi, almost an anti-Nazi, the German commander charged with defense of the city, General von Schwerin, still was regrouping his *116th Panzer Division* north of the city. His depleted forces, he believed, were no match for the Americans bearing down on him. If the fall of Aachen within a few hours was inevitable, Schwerin reasoned, why subject the proud old coronation capital to further destruction?

Entering Aachen around nightfall, Schwerin found the civilian population in a panic. The Nazis, he learned, had ordered all civilians to flee to the east.

To a man who believed the Americans would arrive in a matter of hours and even that the end of the war was not too many days away, this appeared ridiculous. Schwerin promptly sent officers to police headquarters with orders to halt the evacuation, only to learn to his dismay that not only the police but all government and Nazi Party officials already had fled. Not a policeman was to be found. Thoroughly piqued, Schwerin sent his officers into the streets to halt the hegira themselves.

Meanwhile, Schwerin at last came upon one civilian official still at his post, an employee of the telephone service. To this man Schwerin entrusted a letter in Schwerin's own impeccable English to be given to the incoming American commander:

I stopped the absurd evacuation of this town—therefore, I am responsible for the fate of its inhabitants and I ask you . . . to take care of the unfortunate population in a humane way. I am the last German Commanding Officer in the sector of Aachen.

[signed] Schwerin

Unfortunately for Count Gerhard von Schwerin, the order to evacuate Aachen had come from the pen of the *Fuehrer* himself. Also unfortunately for Schwerin, the American commander, General Collins, had no intention of moving immediately into Aachen.

Schwerin had written a letter he would come to rue.

As daylight came the next day, September 13, General Collins still had no authority to make a genuine attack against the Siegfried Line. Displeased by the preceding day's delays, Collins determined nevertheless to make what was in effect a full-scale attack, even though he continued to call it a "reconnaissance in force."

Taking a battalion from the 1st Division to reinforce his armor, he turned the rest of the 1st Division loose to break through the pillbox belt close to Aachen and gain the high ground in a half-moon arc about the city, there to await juncture with the XIX Corps from the north to complete the encirclement. To Maurice Rose of the 3d Armored Division he stressed the necessity of pushing swiftly up the Stolberg

Corridor. Collins directed the 9th Division, which had been two days' march behind the others, to hurry forward to sweep the Huertgen Forest.

To a task force of the 3d Armored Division's Combat Command B, which on September 12 had reached the dragon's teeth near Roetgen, fell the dubious distinction of being the first American unit to enter the Huertgen Forest. Commanded by Lt. Col. William B. Lovelady, a big, robust tank officer, this task force in moving north from Roetgen would pass through a fringe of what became known as the Huertgen Forest before turning northeast up the Stolberg Corridor. Fortunately for Lovelady and the men under him, the Germans were not yet prepared to turn the forest into the cauldron of misery and death it was later to become.

Bulldozers began work at dawn to erase the big crater blocking passage along the main road, but the fill proved too mucky to support the tanks. While the division commander, General Rose, fumed at the delay, engineers eventually had to blast a path through the adjacent dragon's teeth with explosives. Not until almost noon did the first tanks pass.

As the task force proceeded cautiously northward along a highway framed by dense forest, the Germans in a succession of eight pillboxes fled in disorder. The force continued unopposed until the lead tanks reached a village in a clearing, where they were suddenly halted by the fire of a concealed Mark V tank and several antitank guns. In a few blazing minutes the American task force lost four Shermans and a half-track. The Germans held up the column for more than an hour before someone at last drew a bead on the Panther and knocked it out.

Though Task Force Lovelady continued through the village, a demolished bridge discouraged further moves for the day. The task force had covered no great distance—only just over two miles—but the Scharnhorst Line, the thin forward band of the Siegfried Line, lay behind.

Elsewhere, the going was more difficult. Because the 1st Division was still closing up to the border, only one regiment of the infantry got into the fight, and roadblocks, delaying detachments, and small-scale counterattacks thwarted any real effort against the pillboxes themselves. Meanwhile, the 3d Armored Division's Combat Command A, attacking full against the face of the Stolberg Corridor over dangerously open ground between Aachen and Roetgen, ran into the main strength of the enemy's incoming *9th Panzer Division* and its meager but nonetheless troublesome attachments.

Supported by tanks and tank destroyers spewing fire from the edge of a woods, dismounted armored infantrymen of CCA soon after daylight got past the dragon's teeth, only to come to ground in the face of intense machine-gun fire. Artillery could not silence the enemy gunners, and German mortar fire prevented engineers from blowing a path through the dragon's teeth to enable tanks to come to the infantry's aid.

It was mid-afternoon and the attack appeared to have faltered when someone found a cart track near by. Here German farmers had built a fill of stone and earth to provide a path for their wagons across the dragon's teeth. The American task force commander, Col. Leander Doan, quickly ordered his tanks forward.

Lest the Germans had mined the roadway, the tankers sent in the lead a Scorpion, a tank equipped with a device of heavy chains to flail the earth. But the Scorpion quickly mired in the soft earth, and nothing else could get past.

As German gunners awoke to what was happening and began to shell the roadway, hope of breaking into the fortified line might have faded again had not a tank platoon leader, Lt. John R. Hoffman, and the commander of the flail tank, Sgt. Sverry "Weegie" Dahl, braved the fire to hitch two tanks to the Scorpion and pull it from the mud. Climbing back into the flail tank, "Weegie" Dahl gunned the motor for a second try. This time he rumbled across.

As the rest of Colonel Doan's tanks followed, chances of a second penetration of the thin Scharnhorst Line appeared bright. But though few in number, the men of the German *9th Panzer Division* were an intrepid lot. With *Panzerfausts*, they quickly knocked out four of the American tanks, then gained additional heart with the arrival of three assault guns that only a few hours before had been unloaded from a train in Aachen. The assault guns quickly knocked out six of the Shermans. Colonel Doan had only ten tanks left.

In the end, it took reinforcements and the coming of darkness for CCA to turn this foray into the Scharnhorst Line into a penetration. Two fresh platoons of tanks from the combat command's reserve came to Doan's aid, and the division commander, General Rose, sent the attached battalion from the 1st Division. As the approach of darkness restricted German observation from the pillboxes, tanks and infantry together began to advance. In less than an hour they had roared past the last of the pillboxes. Behind a concentrated artillery barrage, they plunged on into the first village beyond the fortified line. Again the total advance was just over two miles, but the first belt of pillboxes lay behind.

Reports of Doan's and Lovelady's penetrations went a long way toward convincing Friedrich-August Schack that penetrating the West Wall, not capturing Aachen, was the immediate American goal. Yet heavy artillery fire on Aachen and presence of apparently strong infantry forces close to the city left him reluctant to move any of General von Schwerin's *116th Panzer Division* from Aachen into the Stolberg Corridor. This despite almost frantic pleas for help from the commander of the *9th Panzer Division*, Generalmajor Gerhard Mueller. Mueller's panzer grenadiers had fought heroically against heavy odds, but they had been no more than a hard crust. Almost nothing remained to deny American exploitation the next day.

All General Schack could send to help was a *Luftwaffe* fortress battalion and a battery of artillery. This obviously would not be enough. Reluctantly, Schack told engineers to begin demolishing bridges over the little Vicht River in front of the Schill Line, the second, thicker band of West Wall defenses.

As daylight came on September 14 and Joe Collins could at last officially label his advance an attack, it became readily apparent that the stanch resistance the preceding day had been about all the enemy could muster for the time being.

The 1st Division on the left at last got a real drive going, quickly penetrated the Scharnhorst Line, and sent a regiment alongside the left flank of the 3d Armored Division. Both attacking combat commands made rapid strides, delayed only briefly by detachments of generally irresolute German riflemen and machine gunners, and roads blocked by craters and hastily built log obstacles. And the 47th Infantry, a regiment of the 9th Division, entered the action for the first time to drive through the fringe of the Huertgen Forest and protect the armor's right flank.

Task Force Lovelady made the most impressive advance. Moving for more than four and a half miles across rolling countryside, the task force by nightfall had gained the Vicht River south of Stolberg. As the demoralized crews of a nest of 88mm. guns overlooking a demolished bridge cringed in terror, Colonel Lovelady sent his armored infantrymen to wade the little river.

The Germans here were members of one of the local-security battalions General Schack had placed under the headquarters of the *353d Infantry Division* to hold the Schill Line. Before daylight the next morning, September 15, the men of the battalion slipped away in the darkness. When Task Force Lovelady's tanks crossed a newly constructed bridge over the Vicht around noon on the fifteenth, the pillboxes of the Schill Line were silent, empty. Two miles beyond the river, the armor passed the last of the fortifications and headed for open country.

The 3d Armored Division's CCB had penetrated the entire Siegfried Line.

More toward the center of the Stolberg Corridor, CCA made comparable progress on September 14 but paused the next morning until infantrymen of the 1st Division could seize high ground off the combat command's left flank, the high ground directly east of Aachen. Heading into the Schill Line northwest of Stolberg around noon, the armor found the going easy as another local-security battalion faded away. Nosing aside an ineffective roadblock made of overturned farm wagons, eight U.S. tanks were moving among the pillboxes when seven concealed assault guns opened fire and quickly knocked out six of the tanks.

It took the rest of the afternoon and another assist from infantry of the 1st Division before the assault guns fled and CCA gained the nest of pillboxes. Yet as the armor coiled for the night, only a few scattered fortifications remained before CCA, like CCB, would be all the way through the Siegfried Line.

From the German viewpoint, CCA's success was all the more distressing because it had broken contact between the *116th Panzer Division* in Aachen and what remained of the *9th Panzer Division* in the Stolberg Corridor. Despite continued advances by the American armor, General Schack still sided with General von Schwerin in the belief that the Americans intended to assault the city. Since American infantry on September 15 had occupied the high ground in a semicircle about Aachen, they obviously planned to move against the city the next day. Aware that Hitler considered himself and his Third Reich the successors to Charlemagne and the Carolingian Empire and thus had enshrined Aachen as a holy place in the National Socialist movement, Schack shuddered at the thought of weakening the city's defenses.

As for Schwerin, he himself had troubles apart from the American threat. The panic which had struck the civilian population the night of September 12 recrudesced during September 14, and with it came a special order from Hitler himself. All civilians, the *Fuehrer* directed, were to be evacuated from Aachen—by force, if necessary. Still convinced that the Americans soon would enter Aachen, reluctant to expose the civilians to the apparently unnecessary hardship of fleeing, Schwerin nevertheless had no choice but to concur.

When police and Nazi officials returned to Aachen on September 15, they found the evacuation again underway, but this was not sufficient to keep Schwerin out of trouble. The letter the general had written to the incoming American commander fell quickly into Nazi hands.

You are relieved of your command, the Nazi officials told Schwerin, to stand trial before Hitler's "People's Court."

Absurd, the fractious Schwerin snorted. Aachen will fall; the war soon will be over.

Of a quick end to the war, Schwerin was certain. As long ago as July he had been so sure the war was lost that he had agreed to serve as emissary to the Allies if the plot to kill Hitler succeeded. Nor was relief from his command anything new to Schwerin. Only a few weeks before, when he had disregarded an order to join in a futile counterattack, his superiors had relieved him, but it had not been long before they relented. Everybody knew how loyal the men of the *116th Panzer Division* were to Schwerin, from whose ancestral landholdings the original cadre for the division had come.

Gathering about him troops of the *116th Panzer Division's Reconnaissance Battalion,* Schwerin took refuge behind a cordon of machine guns in a farmhouse near Aachen. Here he would wait out the imminent fall of the city and the end of the war.

Schwerin must have watched with considerable dismay during the next few days as no further American move against Aachen developed. A week later he established communication with his old friend Field Marshal von Rundstedt, Commander in Chief in the West, and asked help. Rundstedt subsequently interceded with Hitler to shift Schwerin's trial to a military tribunal. In the end, Schwerin got off with little more than a reprimand, a striking commentary either on the advantage of having friends in high places or on the influence still wielded by the old nobility in Nazi Germany.

But command of Schwerin's beloved *116th Panzer Division* passed to another man.

Elsewhere, on September 15, the German corps commander in the Stolberg Corridor in desperation exhorted his subordinate, Gerhard Mueller of the *9th Panzer Division,* to counterattack Task Force Lovelady below Stolberg. This General Mueller patently could not do with the forces available to him, but he still might be able to do real damage to the American force.

As Task Force Lovelady filed past the last pillboxes during

the afternoon of September 15, the open ground facing the armored column lay in a shallow defile, a hill crowned by a factory rising on the left and the skirt of the Huertgen Forest on the right. Lead vehicles were full in the open when six German assault guns opened fire from the flanks, knocking out seven medium tanks and a tank destroyer.

Pulling his troops back to the protection of a village, Colonel Lovelady reported to CCB headquarters that he had only thirteen medium tanks left. Halt for the night, Lovelady recommended; he then could launch a concentrated effort the next morning to take the high ground on his left while the 9th Division's 47th Infantry came abreast in the forest on the right.

Adroit employment of thirteen assault guns thus had dealt telling blows to both CCA and CCB during the afternoon of the fifteenth. Had the 3d Armored Division been at full strength, these would have been mere annoying jabs, easily parried, but the armored division was far from full strength. The blows hurt. What was more, the night's delay they imposed gave the Germans time to muster opposition at the critical points to cause more trouble the next day.

On September 16, the fifth day of the VII Corps attack, both armored combat commands had a bad time of it for the most part, but the day ended on a note of encouragement nonetheless. For even as the armor found the going slow, the 9th Division's 47th Infantry, protecting the right flank of the armor in the fringe of the Huertgen Forest, came up with a surprise advance. After two days of delay and confusion fostered by the trackless forest and one concealed pillbox after another, a battalion of the 47th Infantry suddenly spurted past the last fortifications of the Schill Line. Marching uncontested through the woods, the battalion reached Schevenhuette, a village four miles east of Stolberg, where a few startled Germans threw their hands high in surrender.

The 47th Infantry thus had advanced approximately ten miles into Germany, deeper than any other Allied unit. The regiment stood less than seven miles from the VII Corps objective, the Roer River at the city of Dueren. The success set telephones to ringing high up the chain of command, breathing new life into the First Army's hopes for making a clean breach of the Siegfried Line and continuing the pursuit of the Germans to the Rhine.

On the other hand, down at the fighting man's level, nobody could be quite so elated; for as night came on the sixteenth, disturbing reports began to filter in. Just before dark, for example, a patrol from the 1st Division spotted an enemy column in the distance stretching "as far as the eye can see." Through the night almost every unit along the front noted the noise of heavy motor traffic behind German lines. Most disturbing of all, an outpost of the 47th Infantry at Schevenhuette captured a German colonel on reconnaissance.

Because the colonel was from a unit nobody had heard of before, the *12th Infantry Division*, intelligence officers pondered the meaning of his presence. Wary of counterattack, the 47th Infantry commander, Col. George W. Smythe, canceled his plans for continuing the attack the next morning. Maintain full alert, he warned his men, for whatever might happen when daylight came on September 17.

Well might Colonel Smythe be concerned, for during the sixteenth, events on the German side had taken a distinct turn for the better. First contingents of the eagerly awaited *12th Infantry Division* had arrived at the Roer River, and the entire division was scheduled to be on hand within twenty-four hours.

Napoleon hardly could have produced the Imperial Guard with a more apt sense of timing.

PROLOGUE CONTINUED

5   MONSCHAU LIES at the southwestern tip of the Huert-gen Forest. In peacetime a haven for German honeymoon couples, the village snuggles in a deep gorge on both banks of the Roer River, here near its source a tumbling, gurgling mountain-type stream. So narrow are the streets that through traffic must use a bypass road halfway up the clifflike hill behind the village. Upper stories of ancient houses built of stucco with exposed timber supports overhang the streets.

In September 1944, Monschau itself was of little military importance. What was important in the mind of the VII Corps commander, General Collins, was a high ridgeline southeast of the village. This ground would be useful, Collins believed, for protecting the right flank of the corps, which for fifteen miles lay open except for a thin veil of mechanized cavalry. What was important also was a high, plateaulike clearing some four miles wide stretching for seven miles northeast from Monschau. From this big clearing, studded with villages, two main roads lead northeast, one passing through the village of Huertgen toward Dueren, the other wending more to the east through the crossroads village of Schmidt, which crowns one of the highest ridgelines west of the Roer. This elevated clearing provides the closest thing to a terrain corridor to be found along the southern fringe of the Huertgen Forest.

It was to this plateau—which may be called the Monschau Corridor—and to the ridgeline near Monschau that General Collins ordered the bulk of the 9th Infantry Division. While one regiment guarded the right flank of the armor in the Stolberg Corridor, the other two were to protect the exposed south flank of the VII Corps and sweep the entire expanse of the Huertgen Forest.

It was a tremendous job for a lone infantry division, one markedly inconsonant with the way the 9th Division commander, Maj. Gen. Louis A. Craig, liked to fight a war. More than any of the other VII Corps division commanders, Craig was given to following the sane, sober methods laid down by the army field manuals. Having pursued his career under the shadow of a brother, one of the most indomitable Chiefs of Staff who ever ran the U.S. Army, Craig himself was a soft-spoken man who never drank, never smoked, never swore. At fifty-three years of age, he had stepped down from a corps command in the United States to make sure of seeing combat action.

For all Craig's sane, solid inclinations, he and his 9th Division drew a markedly unorthodox assignment in the attack to pierce the Siegfried Line. Indeed, the task was irreconcilable with the size of the force involved had General Collins looked upon the action as anything more than continued pursuit. The 9th Division's sector was nineteen miles wide, more than three times what an infantry division normally handled, even in unconstricted terrain. Yet pursuit was anticipated everywhere on the front, as evidenced by the fact that the VII Corps sector was 35 miles wide, and that of the First Army more than 120 miles.

That Collins assigned the 9th Division the mission of securing the ridgeline southeast of Monschau demonstrated as much as anything else that nobody expected serious resistance. For even though this ridgeline, topped by the villages of Hoefen and Alzen, is prominent terrain, a number of points on the north side of the Roer River within the Monschau Corridor are higher. However desirable this ridgeline as an outpost for the corridor, hardly anybody would have recommended tying up a major portion of the overextended 9th Division for any appreciable period to secure it.

But that was what happened. The entire 60th Infantry Regiment, one-third of the division, would be involved for five days on the Hoefen–Alzen Ridge at a time when the weight of the regiment might have been decisive elsewhere.

It was not, of course, intended that way. In the first place, the belief that the Germans would make no sharp fight of it appeared based on fact. Here stood Eberhard Roesler's *89th Infantry Division*, the weak northern half of Erich Straube's *74th Corps*. Unfortunately for the 9th Division, the 350 men of the *1056th Regiment*, the only hard core of veterans available to Colonel Roesler, had been assigned to the Hoefen–Alzen Ridge.

Nor did General Craig intend at first to commit the entire 60th Infantry to the task. Only a reinforced battalion, commanded by Lt. Col. Lee W. Chatfield, was scheduled to take the ridge.

Avoiding the obvious attack route directly through Monschau, Chatfield during September 13 circled far to the south to come upon the ridge from the southwest. But the next day hardly had his infantrymen crossed a wooded ravine and emerged on the open ground of the ridge when small arms and machine-gun fire from Siegfried Line pillboxes brought them up sharply. During the evening of the fourteenth, General Craig, in hope of making quick work of the ridge and getting on to the more important task of breaking through the Monschau Corridor, sent the rest of the regiment to help.

Despite a concentric attack, from Monschau and from Chatfield's position southwest of the ridge, it was not until four days later, September 18, that the *1056th Regiment* retired from the Hoefen–Alzen Ridge, and then only after counterattacking with a fury that for a while jeopardized all the 60th Infantry's gains. Whether intentionally or by chance, Colonel Roesler—the commander who had been reduced to towing an Italian artillery piece about his front to simulate artillery strength—had managed to tie up an entire American regiment, one-ninth of the entire attacking force of the VII Corps, for five crucial days.

Louis Craig's remaining regiment, the 39th Infantry, meanwhile could have used considerable help in the Monschau Corridor. Though the *89th Division* had assigned defense of the corridor to some 1,300 men of a grenadier training regiment, the pillboxes of the Scharnhorst Line would put real backbone into the defense. In recognition of the likely avenue of advance provided by the village-studded plateau northeast of Monschau, West Wall engineers here had erected one of the strongest belts of fortifications in the entire forward band.

The leading battalion of the 39th Infantry came up to the dragon's teeth on September 14, even as Colonel Chatfield's men were first striking the Hoefen–Alzen Ridge and as the 47th Infantry was first entering the fight to help the armor up the Stolberg Corridor. Lammersdorf, a village just short of the dragon's teeth, the infantrymen took without firing a shot, but hardly had they emerged from the last houses into the orchards beyond when small-arms and mortar fire from pillboxes clustered about a customs house on the southern fringe of the Huertgen Forest brought them to an abrupt halt. The battalion commander, Lt. Col. Oscar B. Thompson, sent first one then another company to flank the opposition, but darkness came before any part of the battalion could even reach the dragon's teeth. The pillboxes remained inviolate.

Even before Colonel Thompson had exhausted his own resources, the regimental commander, Col. Van H. Bond, committed another battalion on Thompson's right, but this battalion did not reach the dragon's teeth either, as antitank fire, combined with rifle, machine-gun, and mortar fire, stopped not only the infantry but a company of medium tanks that Bond sent to help.

The second day, September 15, as the American armor in the Stolberg Corridor was penetrating the second band of the Siegfried fortifications, men of the 39th Infantry for the first time developed close co-ordination with their supporting weapons. Reducing the pillboxes nevertheless remained a slow, costly task. In many cases, fire from tanks and tank destroyers dazed the German defenders, but infantrymen still had to work their way close to the apertures of the pillboxes and throw in hand grenades before the Germans gave up. This served to reduce seven pillboxes, but it in no sense punctured the entire line.

During the afternoon, Colonel Bond sent his reserve battalion far around to the north to pass through the fringe of the Huertgen Forest and come upon the troublesome customs-house position in a wide envelopment, but night came again before the battalion reached the rear of the enemy strongpoint. It required tedious, costly small-unit fighting all the next day, September 16—the same day that the 39th Infantry's sister regiment achieved its noteworthy advance to Schevenhuette —before all the pillboxes in the customs-house position fell.

Reduction of these fortifications brought a genuine penetration of the Scharnhorst Line, yet the gap was only a mile and a half wide and could not be exploited, because of the strong fortifications still standing to the south. Some of the highest ground on the entire plateau lay to the south, particularly Hill 554, not quite a mile and a half from Lammersdorf. Anything that moved through Lammersdorf did so only at the will of whoever held Hill 554.

To the 9th Division commander, General Craig, it was apparent by nightfall of September 16 that the 39th Infantry alone could not even push through the Monschau Corridor, much less clear the sprawling Huertgen Forest. All three battalions of the regiment already were in the line, all seriously understrength from the ravages of the pursuit and the early pillbox fighting. Nor was assistance to be expected from the 47th Infantry at Schevenhuette, separated by more than seven miles of dense forest from the rest of the division. Though Craig hoped that the 60th Infantry would soon be available to help, not for another two days was this regiment to eliminate the last of the enemy from the Hoefen-Alzen Ridge.

The first five days of fighting in the Siegfried Line had brought the VII Corps few spectacular successes. Indeed, German commanders considered the American advance a timid, exploratory probe and wondered what kept the Americans from making an all-out effort. Was the residue of German propaganda about the impregnability of the West Wall still powerful enough, pondered the *Seventh Army* commander, General Brandenberger, to prompt the enemy to reorganize before making a full-scale attack? Had the early efforts of the weak German forces so impressed the enemy that he would wait to close ranks? Or was it simply a matter of supplies?

Just how much of the failure to achieve a rapid, full-scale penetration of the Siegfried Line was attributable to awe is difficult to pin down, even after observing the operations from the American side. Yet awe obviously had something to do with the nature of the attack. There were other factors as well. With tanks worn out by the pursuit, Maurice Rose's 3d Armored Division had attacked with tank strength equivalent to little more than one tank battalion. Apart from limited numbers of tanks and tank destroyers, the U.S. troops had arrived ill equipped for assaulting a fortified line. Coming upon the pillboxes at the end of a long pursuit, they had at hand few prepared demolition charges, Bangalore torpedoes (lengths of pipe filled with explosives), flamethrowers, or other special equipment. Alternating haze and light rain at the same time had denied major contribution by tactical aircraft. Units were understrength, the men tired, and by nightfall of the sixteenth every major combat unit of the VII Corps was in the line, stretched to the limit. With the V Corps engaged deep in the Ardennes–Eifel and the XIX Corps fighting to reach the Siegfried Line north of Aachen, the First Army commander, General Hodges, had nothing to send to help. What was more, ammunition was dangerously low, particularly for the artillery's main weapon, the 105mm. howitzer.

Yet for all the seemingly groping nature of the advance, bearing little apparent resemblance to Joe Collins' early expectations, the VII Corps still had pierced the forward band of the Siegfried Line on a front of over eleven miles and had achieved in the second belt two penetrations. Furthermore, the Germans had provided no real evidence that they could move up major reinforcements.

On the German side, the *89th Division*, for all its success in the Monschau Corridor and on the Hoefen–Alzen Ridge, still had to rely for artillery support upon antitank guns and mortars. Neither the *116th Panzer Division* at Aachen nor the *9th Panzer Division* in the Stolberg Corridor had been shored up appreciably. Convinced that the *9th Panzer Division* commander, General Mueller, had failed to maintain adequate control of his conglomerate formations, Brandenberger, the army commander, relieved both Mueller and his chief of staff.

Transferring all responsibility for the Stolberg Corridor to a residual commander of the panzer division, Brandenberger told the commander of the *353d Infantry Division,* Generalleutnant Paul Mahlmann, to take whoever had survived the unsuccessful efforts to hold the Schill Line and move into the Huertgen Forest. Here, with Straube's *74th Corps,* he was to defend the forest from Schevenhuette to the boundary, under Straube's command. Thus the entire Huertgen Forest became the responsibility of Erich Straube, a wrinkled, wizened little man, at fifty-seven older than most German corps and division commanders.

In the meantime, all through the night of the sixteenth, Brandenberger's main hope for thwarting the American attack, the fresh *12th Infantry Division,* continued to arrive at railroad stations along the Roer River. Numbering 14,800 men, the *12th Division* had an antitank battalion with twelve 75mm. guns, its entire complement of artillery—nine batteries of 105's and three batteries of 150's—and seventeen assault guns.

To German soldiers and civilians alike, the *12th Infantry Division* was a welcome, heartening, even exhilarating sight.

Of the American units in the Stolberg Corridor scheduled to attack on September 17, only the 47th Infantry at Schevenhuette deferred to the indications during the night of something stirring behind German lines. Both Combat Commands A and B of the 3d Armored Division were getting ready to expand their penetrations of the Schill Line when the Germans struck.

Northwest of Stolberg, a heavy artillery preparation began shortly before dawn. In well-disciplined waves, bayonets fixed, a battalion of *12th Division* infantrymen plunged toward the seam between CCA and the easternmost battalion of the 1st Division.

Had the Germans moved a few minutes earlier, they might have achieved the full surprise they sought. As it was, the fast-breaking dawn silhouetted them against the sky, posing perfect targets for American artillery and mortar concentrations. Even those who penetrated the shellfire fell or wavered before determined small-arms fire from American foxholes. Not until the afternoon were the German infantrymen able to rally for another try, this one even more disastrous than the first. In a day's fighting, half a regiment was lost, while the Americans, relatively secure in their foxholes, incurred only twenty-three casualties. All the Germans accomplished was to prevent CCA from attacking.

It was much the same southeast of Stolberg, where two more battalions of the *12th Division* hit CCB. Though neither side was ready to attack before midday, the timing of their strikes coincided. Neither force could make real headway.

Meanwhile, another German battalion tried to retake Schevenhuette, the point of deepest American penetration beyond the Siegfried Line. Here the 47th Infantry's Colonel Smythe, a former West Point quarterback, had decided, in effect, to punt on third down, to postpone his attack until he could determine what the Germans were about.

In mid-morning, a patrol under Staff Sgt. Harold Hellerich spotted a German force moving across open ground toward the village. Alerting his company commander by radio, Sergeant Hellerich and his men opened fire. As they pinned the Germans to the ground, gunners in the 47th Infantry's main positions raked the field with machine-gun, mortar, and artillery fire. Of some 200 Germans, no more than ten got away.

To the *12th Division* commander, Col. Gerhard Engel, holder of the Knight's Cross, his nation's highest award for valor, the first day of his division's commitment was thoroughly disheartening. The corps commander, Engel was convinced, had thrust his troops too hurriedly into the line and had scattered their efforts in piecemeal, unco-ordinated attacks. Pointing to the heavy casualties his battalions had absorbed—one was down to a fifth of original strength—Engel asked, almost demanded, permission to postpone further strikes until he could reorganize and prepare a concentrated thrust.

General Schack, the corps commander, had not much choice. In Engel, he had received an ambitious young officer of thirty-eight who had served formerly as an adjutant on Hitler's personal staff, and there were those who said that Hitler himself had anointed Engel with command of the *12th Division* for this critical operation. Schack reluctantly agreed to a pause.

To the American corps commander, General Collins, September 17 brought similar discouragement. Though his men had held firm everywhere, it was obvious that as long as the Germans had reserves and he had none—a strange paradox at this stage of the war—he could not exploit the Siegfried Line penetrations. Until this could be remedied, he told Maurice Rose to confine his 3d Armored Division's attacks to linking the two penetrations of the Schill Line. The 1st Division was to await juncture with the XIX Corps, scheduled to encircle Aachen from the north, and then was to take the city. The 9th Division, meanwhile, was to clear the Huertgen Forest between Schevenhuette and Monschau.

Collins was doing nothing more than anticipating at his level of command what Courtney Hodges the same day had begun to prepare for at army level. Not only Collins' VII Corps but also Gerow's V Corps had bogged down in the first, widespread attempt to pierce the border fortifications. Though the opposition these corps encountered was not really disturbing, it was sufficient to discourage hopes for an immediate breakthrough on a broad front. Consolidation obviously was indispensable, after which a new, concentrated thrust should be launched, Hodges believed, in the Aachen sector.

By adroit use of their meager forces, the Germans of the *Seventh Army*, with the help of the West Wall, the harsh terrain, and the gross overextension of their adversary, had acquired a measure of time that six days before the most optimistic among them could hardly have considered possible. Not that the long-range danger or even the immediate threat was over. No one was more conscious than the sober, methodical General Brandenberger of the onrush of the XIX U.S. Corps north of Aachen and of the continuing over-all superiority of Allied forces. But no one could deny that for the moment the situation was not so utterly hopeless as it had been that gloomy night nearly a week ago when it appeared that the Americans had beaten the *2d Panzer Division* into the pillboxes—the same night, in fact, that Aachen might have been had for the taking.

Nor was there any belief on the American side that the delay was anything more than temporary. Taking leave of the V Corps to fly to Washington to testify in a congressional investigation, Leonard Gerow told his men he expected the war would be over before he got back. The same day that the *12th Division* appeared in the Stolberg Corridor, three Allied airborne divisions came to earth in The Netherlands in the war's largest airborne assault. They were supposed to gain a bridgehead across the lower reaches of the Rhine River, outflank the entire Siegfried Line, and set the stage for a rapid thrust across the north German plain, possibly to Berlin.

The great pursuit, those on the Allied side believed, was far from over.

THE GLOOM AND THE MISERY: THE 9TH DIVISION

6 To conform with Joe Collins' plan to consolidate gains before renewing a major thrust, Louis Craig of the 9th Division had to adopt a new approach to the Huertgen Forest. Heretofore, the object had been to break the Siegfried Line in the Monschau Corridor, then turn northeast up the main highway through the village of Huertgen, sweeping the forest in the process. Reflecting the general awareness that the Germans had mustered a considerable, however motley, defensive force along the border, the new object was to push directly east through the forest to Huertgen. The widely separated thrusts of the 39th and 47th Regiments thus might be welded together to create a solid front for the 9th Division.

Because the new order coincided roughly with completion of the 60th Infantry's conquest of the Hoefen–Alzen Ridge below Monschau, General Craig had a force at hand to take on the new assignment. As corps cavalry assumed responsibility for holding the ridgeline, Craig left behind one of the 60th Infantry's battalions as a reserve and directed the rest of the regiment to penetrate the thick forest. To make up for the battalion left behind, he withdrew Colonel Thompson's 1st Battalion, 39th Infantry, from the Monschau Corridor and attached it to the 60th Infantry.

The 39th Infantry, reduced now in strength by one-third,

was left to fight alone to secure the penetration of the Scharnhorst Line at Lammersdorf. For the rest of the month of September the two remaining battalions of this regiment were
destined to fight almost without pause in quest of two dominating pieces of ground needed to guarantee the break in the
belt of pillboxes. One of these was Hill 554, a mile and a half
southeast of Lammersdorf. The other was a high ridge crowned
by the village of Rollesbroich, which looks down from the east
on the ground about Lammersdorf.

Seriously depleted—one company was down to sixty men,
another to eighty, far from the normal rifle company strength
of 180—both battalions fought doggedly. But so did the Germans. Surrounded, a group in one pillbox refused to surrender
even after men of Company I set off explosive charges against
the steel door. The company commander finally called in a
tankdozer (a tank equipped with a bulldozer blade) to cover
the entrance of the pillbox with earth. Still the Germans refused to surrender. In the end the tankdozer sealed the entrance and all firing embrasures, burying the men alive.

By this time the American units had developed closely
co-ordinated patterns of maneuver against the fortifications.
While mortars and artillery, or tanks and tank destroyers,
opened fire to drive the defenders from foxholes and trenches
into the pillbox itself, some five to eight men inched their way
forward. As the men neared the pillbox, supporting fire lifted.
The men charged, tossing grenades into firing apertures or
blowing in the pillbox door with charges of TNT. Sometimes
they used instead a rocket from an antitank bazooka or dropped
fiery white phosphorus grenades down ventilator shafts. When
finally cornered, the Germans usually surrendered. "*Kamerad!*"
they yelled frantically from the pillbox, or thrust an improvised white flag from a firing slot.

The big problem was getting close enough to the pillbox
in the face of a fury of small-arms and mortar fire from
adjacent German positions, some of which were hard to locate.
Solving it involved getting tanks or tank destroyers onto
ground from which they could pin the defenders to the pillboxes and at the same time avoid the deadly fire from concealed German guns.

At best, reducing the fortifications was a slow, costly, painful process.

Late on September 19, hope for a break came when infantry supported by tanks plunged suddenly almost two miles from Lammersdorf toward the high ground beyond before the Germans in Rollesbroich awoke to the threat and opened fire. Fatigued, their numbers depleted, the infantrymen could not get across the last few hundred yards of open ground into the village. Rollesbroich and the dominating ground around it remained in German hands.

Hill 554 southeast of Lammersdorf resisted a whole series of attacks. Though a platoon of the 39th Infantry's Company L got onto the crest at one point, a quick German counterattack supported by three assault guns sent the platoon reeling back down the slope. On clear days American planes joined the assault but without notable effect. A flanking maneuver against the hill by two companies also failed until late on September 29, sixteen days after leading contingents of the 39th Infantry had first come up to the dragon's teeth. On this day a co-ordinated thrust by all three rifle companies, supported by tanks concealed behind a smoke screen, at last carried the height.

In the meantime, the 60th Infantry's drive to push directly through the Huertgen Forest to a clearing about the village of Huertgen had begun ten days before, on September 19. This, more than the continuing attacks in the corridor, was the focal point for the 9th Division, for a quick penetration of the forest would enable the division to participate in a new push to the east, even without control of the corridor.

The 60th Infantry planned a two-battalion attack. The attached 1st Battalion, 39th Infantry, commanded by Colonel Thompson, was to move through the center of the forest to seize Huertgen and two nearby villages. This would establish the battalion only just over two miles from the 47th Infantry at Schevenhuette. At the same time, Lee Chatfield's battalion of the 60th Infantry was to pass through a high wooded marsh known as the *Todten Bruch*, or Deadman's Moor, and cut the Lammersdorf–Huertgen highway at the village of Germeter, two miles south of Huertgen.

On the first two days, Thompson's men had as much trouble with the dense woods and steep slopes as with the enemy, but by nightfall of the second day, September 20, they had reached a network of trails in the valley of the Weisser Weh Creek, a stream meandering north through the forest less than a mile from the woods line overlooking Huertgen.

The Germans here had yet to form a firm line. Such units as there were had come under the control of General Mahlmann's *353d Infantry Division* as recently as the night of the sixteenth, after Brandenberger, the *Seventh Army* commander, had shifted Mahlmann's headquarters from the Stolberg Corridor. Yet as daylight came on the twenty-first, Mahlmann sent one small unit after another to harass the American battalion until he could muster a larger force to make a real counterattack. To Colonel Thompson, who was trying to get tanks and tank destroyers forward over muddy trails and firebreaks, these small thrusts made it clear that he needed strong fire support before moving from the forest into Huertgen.

Thompson's men had just finished a hasty breakfast of K rations the next morning, September 22, when word came from the division commander, General Craig, to hold fast. At Schevenhuette, the enemy's *12th Infantry Division* had counterattacked the 47th Infantry again, this time with grim determination. Both Thompson's men and the 60th Infantry's reserve battalion, Craig directed, were to hurry north, lest the Germans eliminate the advanced position at Schevenhuette.

As events developed, neither of the two battalions had to be used at Schevenhuette, but the threat there had served to erase the promising penetration toward Huertgen. By the time Thompson's men were able to return three days later, on September 25, the *353d Division* had occupied the wooded slopes of the Weisser Weh valley in strength. What was more, Thompson's battalion could not repeat the original assignment but again had to go to the aid of a neighboring unit. This time it was Lee Chatfield's battalion deep in the forest on the high ground in Deadman's Moor. Chatfield needed help, needed it badly.

Even though other battalions had gone before into the

forest, Colonel Chatfield's 1st Battalion, 6oth Infantry, was the
first in what was destined to be a long procession of American
units that would come to know the full gloom, misery, and
physical and moral abrasion of the way of fighting and dying
called Huertgen Forest. Like some amorphous leech, the forest
sucked at the lifeblood of a man's body and spirit. To a man
in the ranks, it seemed that nobody knew where he was going
except the enemy, who through some sixth sense was capable
of exploiting every stinking inch of the forest to fullest
advantage.

"The enemy seemed to be everywhere," one man recalled,
"and in the darkness of the thick trees and the confusion, the
firing seemed everywhere."

"If anybody says he knew where he was in the forest,"
said another, a battalion commander, "he's a liar."

Under a dense curtain of rain-heavy fir branches, across
a spongy cushion of wet brown droppings from the firs, a man
moved cautiously from one tree trunk to another. Each step
might be his last. Even if the spewings of the burp-gun that
might erupt at any moment from deep within the trees happened to miss you, it caught the man beside you, or the man
six paces to the right or eight paces to the left. Next time you
might be the one.

It was misery from the start. As men of the 1st Battalion
unloaded from trucks in the fringe of the forest before daylight on September 20, the rain poured with an evil persistence.
Even those who somehow had held on to their raincoats
through the bitter fighting on the Hoefen–Alzen Ridge found
them little protection. So dark was the night that it seemed
one might cut chunks of it with a knife. Like sheep, the men
huddled together, wondering how far away were the Germans,
longing for a look at a sky they had failed to appreciate before
the heavy firs snatched it away, yearning for a cigarette but
daring not.

The mission, as it came down from company and platoon
commanders who somehow found their way through the darkness to the side of the battalion commander and back again,
was glibly enough put. They were to attack southeast, seizing

first Deadman's Moor. Then they were to turn northeast to Germeter. Though the attack was not to begin until an hour after midday, they were supposed to arrive in Germeter by 1800 (6 P.M.) the same day. As clearly indicated by the time-table, resistance was expected to be "negligible," as the trite military phraseology of the day would have it. An occasional block of felled trees across trail or firebreak, perhaps, defended by irresolute Germans who had no stomach for a fight.

The question was, Who believed it?

But as the advance began, it looked for a while as if the dubious would find their skepticism unfounded. Moving cautiously through the woods alongside a road that wends southeastward to a juncture with the Lammersdorf–Huertgen highway near a woodchopper's hut called Jaegerhaus, the leading company picked off one undefended pillbox after another as if they were beads on a string. The company was, in effect, rolling up the second band of the Siegfried Line, the Schill Line, with not a German in sight. More than one man was becoming convinced that, for once, those who gave the orders might have known what they were talking about, that resistance would, after all, be "negligible."

Then up ahead the lead scouts signaled caution.

Almost at the same moment a German machine gun opened fire.

As the men hit the ground and began to build up a firing line, word passed back that the scouts had come on a block of felled trees at the crossing of two firebreaks. Colonel Chatfield, the battalion commander, promptly ordered the lead company to hold in place while Company B tried to flank the position. But hardly had Company B begun to move when it too came under fire from a cleverly camouflaged pillbox.

The true battle of the Huertgen Forest had started.

It took most of the rest of the afternoon for Company B to pin the defenders inside the pillbox with small-arms fire, work gradually up to within hand-grenade range of them, and force them to surrender. In the process, Company B's commander and all his command group were either killed or wounded.

The marshy, wooded ridgeline, not to mention the village of Germeter, remained out of reach all that day and the next. Only on the third day, September 22, after a platoon of tank destroyers had worked forward over boggy ground to provide fire support against the pillboxes, was substantial progress made. With the destroyers threading through the trees like clumsy, noisy ducks, a renewed attack by mid-afternoon had cleared all the ridge except for one pillbox just over the crest on the eastern slope. Here the bulk of Company C was pinned down by small-arms fire when the Germans struck back.

First indication that the Germans were preparing to counterattack came from a prisoner whom few in the 1st Battalion, 60th Infantry, were inclined to doubt. By remarkable coincidence, the German and the battalion's intelligence officer had lived as neighbors years before in Germany when both were children.

In the event, there was little time to doubt the prisoner. Hardly had he revealed the plan when German machine guns and mortars opened fire. Through the woods poured a wave of German infantry.

As had happened five days before in the Stolberg Corridor, the complexion of the fight changed in the Huertgen Forest. It changed because the *74th Corps* commander, Erich Straube, a man whose bravery had been attested to by an award of the Knight's Cross but a man who grew nervous under crisis nevertheless, had yelled for help. Though Brandenberger, the army commander, found it hard to believe the Americans would make a major thrust through the inhospitable forest, he shifted an assault gun brigade from the Stolberg Corridor to give Straube a hand. Around this brigade, equipped with six guns, General Mahlmann of the *353d Division* had assembled a battalion each of infantry and engineers, an artillery battery, and five antitank guns.

Though the counterattack the afternoon of September 22 gained no ground, intense combat at hand-grenade range raged back and forth along the wooded ridge for the next three days. Here and there the Germans, emerging unannounced through some undefended portion of the forest, forced Colonel Chatfield to hurry a company or a platoon or a squad to thwart their advance. In less than two days, Chatfield's units had become thoroughly intermingled. Company commanders and even platoon leaders often did not know in the confusion of the forest what men or how many men they commanded. Shells from mortars or the enemy's self-propelled guns exploded high in the treetops, raining thousands of deadly metal fragments upon the foxholes below. The platoon of lightly armored American tank destroyers fired back in turn, all the while hugging the thin line of riflemen for protection from Germans roaming the woods with *Panzerfausts*.

The fighting centered on possession of a nest of three pillboxes that changed hands time after time. At one point, the Germans overran one of the pillboxes in a night attack and captured forty-nine men, including all four officers and the command group of Company A. Only thirty riflemen remained. Although a few wide-eyed individual replacements arrived, neither this company nor the others managed to average more than about fifty riflemen each actually on the firing line. When at one point Colonel Chatfield ordered Company B to retake a pillbox, the company commander defied him. His company, he said, was too weak to move. When Chatfield summarily relieved the officer of his command, Company B went on to gain the pillbox; but the fact remained that all the companies now were perilously understrength.

To the Americans it seemed that the Germans had an apparently inexhaustible supply of men to send against them and that all advantage lay with the enemy. That this could appear to be the case when the German force actually was makeshift was a testimony to the forest itself as a weapon for the defense. Even errant Germans with little inclination to fight, in wandering through the forest and coming suddenly upon an American supply party toiling over the porous ground with a heavy load of rations or ammunition, might add to the over-all impression of German strength. When daylight came one morning, one company found sixty Germans of a *Luftwaffe* fortress battalion sitting in the woods waiting for a chance to surrender; but when they gave up, no one noted any lessening of German strength.

The truth was that since the Americans were a lone battalion without neighbors to the right or left, the Germans were free to eddy all about them, unseen among the dense trees. Though a liaison plane hovered over the forest to direct artillery fire on Germans moving on roads or trails, the enemy quickly learned to avoid the openings in the woods when the plane was aloft. At the times when the Germans were attacking and American superiority in artillery might have made a real difference, so closely locked were the combatants that the shells would have been unable to distinguish friend from foe.

At first there was little anybody could do to help. The only two battalions that might possibly have been used had been sent north to back up the 47th Infantry at Schevenhuette.

Finally, on September 24, one of these battalions returned to go in on Chatfield's left, but the forest quickly began to exercise its terrible powers of attrition on this unit as well. Hardly had the rifle companies attacked when the Germans struck at a pillbox housing the battalion command post. Only the fire of a tank destroyer, left behind in the event of just such an emergency, plus the fire from rifles, carbines, and pistols of every man the headquarters could muster, finally forced the Germans back. The rifle companies meanwhile could make no appreciable gains.

By September 26, with Thompson's battalion of the 39th Infantry also having returned from Schevenhuette and moved to relieve Chatfield's depleted battalion, the division commander, General Craig, had despaired either of cutting the Lammersdorf–Huertgen highway at Germeter or of taking Huertgen. All he could hope for now was to clear Deadman's Moor and continue south past Jaegerhaus, the woodchopper's hut, to link with the 39th Infantry in the Monschau Corridor. In this manner a solid line might yet be established by at least two of the 9th Division's widely separated regiments.

Even this severely modified plan the depleted force in the Huertgen Forest could not see through to the end. Five days later, the 60th Infantry at last gained the Lammersdorf–Huertgen highway near Jaegerhaus, still a long way from the 39th Infantry in the Monschau Corridor, but even this short gain cost the attacking battalions dearly. It was a wearying and frustrating experience: counterattack following every attack; Germans infiltrating in the night into defensive perimeters; enemy patrols ambushing supply parties; mortar and artillery shells snapping branches and tops from the thick firs as if they were toothpicks and killing or maiming the men underneath.

As September closed, no part of the 60th Infantry or the attached battalion from the 39th Infantry was in any condition either to continue into the Monschau Corridor or to resume the attack toward Huertgen. Almost a thousand men had fallen in the grim forest fighting.

Again the Germans had thrown in a fresh force at a critical point to gain invaluable time. Nineteen days after the first patrol crossed the German border, the Americans still had achieved no major breach of the West Wall fortifications.

Everywhere along the front facing the First Army there was relative quiet as the month came to an end. For reasons the Germans could not understand, the XIX U.S. Corps had failed to attack the West Wall north of Aachen. Now, when the Americans did attack, they would find in the pillboxes the second of the fresh infantry divisions Hitler had promised for the Aachen sector. Nor had the Americans yet made any attack against Aachen itself. In the Stolberg Corridor, once the *12th Infantry Division*'s all-out attempt to retake Schevenhuette had failed, both sides had allowed the fighting to lapse into little more than patrol clashes. General Brandenberger thus had been able to relinquish control of both the *9th* and *116th Panzer Divisions* to *Army Group B* so that the armored units might withdraw for rest and refitting.

On the American side, the First Army commander, General Hodges, still had been able to achieve little concentration for renewing the drive to the Rhine. Because the elongated front in the Ardennes–Eifel remained a First Army responsibility, the divisions of Leonard Gerow's V Corps could make only minor shifts northward to reduce the frontage of Collins' VII Corps. Approaching the Siegfried Line north of Aachen, General Corlett's XIX Corps had fallen unhappy heir to an exposed north flank more than thirty miles long which had developed after the British had driven northward into The

Netherlands rather than northeastward alongside the First Army. This open flank took on disturbing proportions after the big airborne assault to assist the British advance fell short of a bridgehead over the lower reaches of the Rhine River and far short of outflanking the Siegfried Line.

Only in the impending arrival of three veteran divisions that had been fighting to reduce a stubborn German hold-out in the port of Brest, far back in France, was there promise of substantially augmenting the First Army. Once these divisions arrived, one might cover the exposed north flank of the XIX Corps while the others assumed the defensive job in the Ardennes–Eifel.

Only then could Gerow's V Corps move north and Collins' VII Corps consolidate.

SCHMIDT AND THE
ROER RIVER DAMS

7 For all the hard fighting along the frontier, as September fused into October few commanders on the Allied side saw the scowling new face the Germans had begun to exhibit as anything more than a mask. The big airborne attack in Holland had fallen short of a bridgehead across the Lower Rhine; the First Army had ground to a halt at Aachen; and the Third Army in Lorraine and the Seventh U.S. and First French Armies in Alsace were finding the going equally slow. But this was less a testimony to German resurgence than to Allied weaknesses, which might well have been expected as logical outgrowths of the logistical problems and the tactical dispersion imposed by the pursuit. Though few commanders now anticipated any immediate, dramatic end to the war, they believed nonetheless that once the supply difficulties could be overcome and divisions could be concentrated at critical points, a new thrust would carry at least as far as the Rhine.

Nobody believed this any more firmly than did Courtney Hodges of the First Army and Joe Collins of the VII Corps. Having considered some pause at or just beyond the German border almost inevitable, they nevertheless had managed to penetrate the Siegfried Line before a pause became imperative. Knowing at first hand how tired and depleted were the divisions and how meager their ammunition and gasoline supply, Hodges and Collins saw no evidence that the kind of opposition the Germans had mustered could continue to prove effective once the U.S. divisions were rested, reinforced, and adequately supplied.

Guided by this kind of thinking and by the expectation that the three divisions from Brittany might soon arrive, Hodges late on September 29 ordered a new drive to reach the Rhine. The offensive was to begin on the second day of October as the XIX Corps launched its long-delayed attack to break the Siegfried Line north of Aachen and drive to the Roer River. Encirclement of Aachen completed as a corollary of this attack, the 1st Division was to reduce the city while the 3d Armored and 9th Divisions, the latter passing through the Huertgen Forest, went on to the Roer. At the same time, Gerow's V Corps below Monschau was to drive northeast across a rugged but relatively shallow corner of the Eifel to outflank the obstacle of the Roer River and gain a bridgehead on the Cologne Plain.

Though Hodges would have preferred all three corps to attack simultaneously, his plan was wedded to the progress of the XIX Corps in the Siegfried Line attack and to the arrival of the divisions from Brittany. In the meantime, General Craig's 9th Division was to get on with the task of clearing the Huertgen Forest.

For the 9th Division the new plan meant more than the mere linking of its three dispersed regiments—the 47th Infantry at Schevenhuette, the 60th Infantry in the forest, and the 39th Infantry in the Monschau Corridor. It meant seizing as a first step the crossroads village of Schmidt, which lies spreadeagled in a big clearing three and a half miles southeast of Huertgen atop one of the highest ridges west of the Roer. With Schmidt and its commanding ground in hand, the bulk of the division might turn north through Huertgen to converge with the 3d Armored Division at Dueren.

To both Joe Collins and his superior, Courtney Hodges, capturing Schmidt would provide the basis for a solution to the enigma that the Huertgen Forest threatened to become. They feared the forest for one basic reason. Both were veterans of the Meuse–Argonne Campaign of World War I, when a German counterattack from the Argonne Forest had been a real and disturbing possibility, and, they were reluctant to ignore the Huertgen Forest, lest the Germans use it as a base for striking into the flank of the First Army's main forces in the Aachen Gap.

Capturing Schmidt meant gaining control of high ground that commanded almost all major crossings of the Roer River upstream from Dueren. Thus, holding Schmidt would provide the means to prevent major enemy forces moving into the Huertgen Forest. Capturing Schmidt also would expose from the rear the stubborn pillbox defenses in the Monschau Corridor, which constituted a kind of fortified redan pricking the VII Corps flank. Once these pillboxes were reduced, the entire south flank of the corps would be pegged firmly on the upper reaches of the Roer from Monschau to Schmidt.

At this stage in the fighting, Collins and Hodges also believed that the Huertgen Forest could be had pretty much for the asking. In view of the harsh experiences of Lee Chatfield's battalion of the 60th Infantry, their thinking might appear at first glance specious, but Chatfield's had been a lone, understrength battalion in a jungle over seven miles wide, exposed to everything the Germans could muster. The voices of a few officers in the 9th Division, impressed by the troubles Chatfield had encountered, went unheeded. They believed the best course would be to attack from the 47th Infantry's positions at Schevenhuette to cut in behind the rear of the forest.

At the beginning of October, the 9th Division intelligence officer, Maj. Jack A. Houston, told his commander that German strength from Schevenhuette to Lammersdorf totaled no more than 5,000 men. They had no firm regimental organization and probably only loose and ineffective division control. Although leadership was for the most part excellent, Houston observed, morale in the ranks was low.

To German commanders, the American concern about the Huertgen Forest was inexplicable. In the first place, contrary to what Hodges and Collins feared, the Germans had no major reserves to mass, least of all strong armored reserves, which would be essential if any damaging blow was to be administered from the forest. In the second place, the Huertgen Forest was hardly a place for armor, even were it available. The few roads and trails could be too readily blocked by a few felled trees and mines covered by a handful of riflemen. Neither Brandenberger, the *Seventh Army* commander, nor Straube, the *74th Corps* commander, could understand why the Americans did not block the roads inside the western fringe of the forest and bypass the forest itself.

Confronted with the reality of American attack, Brandenberger nevertheless had to do what he could to shore up his forest defenses. As soon as the fresh infantry division arrived to occupy the West Wall north of Aachen, he sent the remnants of the old division from that sector into the Huertgen Forest. This was the *275th Infantry Division* under Generalleutnant Hans Schmidt. A physically robust man, Schmidt was level-headed and never rattled under fire. Thus he was to complement Straube, the corps commander, who in time of crisis needed a steady hand near by. Schmidt also was a superb organizer, just the man to mold together the heterogeneous units that had been thrown piece by piece into the forest. As the end of September brought a lull in the forest fighting, Brandenberger ordered Schmidt to take command of both the combat troops and the sector of the *353d Division*. General Mahlmann and the headquarters and support troops of the *353d* he pulled out of the line as the nucleus for building a new division, which was destined to pay a return visit to the forest more than a month later. Thus, General Schmidt, a man who bore the same name as the 9th Division's objective, became responsible for the entire Huertgen Forest.

In many respects, the true condition of the Germans in the forest was much as the 9th Division's Major Houston presumed. By October 3, when absorption of the *353d Division* was complete, Schmidt's *275th Division* had a combat strength of 5,000 men, plus an additional 1,500 men in headquarters and service units. Regimental organization was, as Houston believed, shaky, but improving. As reserves, Schmidt had three battalions totaling 1,200 men. For artillery support, he had a dozen light howitzers and six assault guns.

On the other hand, Major Houston and other American intelligence officers were engaging in the dangerous game of killing off the German army on paper, without regard for the advantage an obstacle like the Huertgen Forest might lend to any force, no matter how disorganized and depleted. While the September fighting had eliminated many of the pillboxes in the forest, quite a few still remained near Germeter, and thick logs available for cutting were ideal for constructing dug-in bunkers and covered foxholes. The German soldier, always adept at digging and building, pitched in with a will under the impetus of both impending attack and the coming cold autumn rains. The German line followed generally the eastern slope of the Weisser Weh Creek valley, roughly in the center of the forest, with strong outposts and roadblocks located farther west.

The 275th Division's mission, as Hans Schmidt interpreted it, was to deny access to the high clearings near the Roer that overlook flatlands of the Cologne Plain leading to the Rhine. Schmidt believed that the clearing around Huertgen was the most important, for here was the nexus of several good roads leading to the Roer and open country at Dueren.

Paradoxically, as both sides prepared for the first set attack in the Huertgen Forest, neither adversary fully appreciated the one really critical objective that the forest concealed. This was a series of dams on the upper reaches of the Roer and its tributaries which later would come to be known as the "Roer River Dams." Whoever held these dams could control the level of the Roer River to the north, downstream from the dams.

The two principal dams in the complex, the Urft and the Schwammenauel, were designed both to provide hydroelectric power and to regulate the Roer. Constructed after the turn of the century on the Urft River, a tributary of the Roer, the concrete Urft Dam can impound approximately 42,000 acre-feet of water. Built in the mid-thirties on the Roer southeast of Schmidt, the earthen Schwammenauel creates a reservoir encompassing about 81,000 acre-feet. Not quite a quarter of a mile wide, the waters of the big Schwammenauel reservoir extend more than three miles upstream from the dam.

In September and October 1944, the existence of the dams was no secret. One had only to turn to Baedecker's regional guide to learn how the eye of the tourist would be struck by the immense size of the dams and by the beauty of the waters in their rustic woodland setting. Yet consulting Baedecker was hardly necessary, for the detailed terrain maps used by both Germans and Americans plainly showed the dams and the reservoir.

Nor was the possible military impact of the dams fully lost on the Americans. "Bank overflows and destructive flood waves," warned the 9th Division's Major Houston, "can be produced by regulating the discharge from the various dams." Houston went on to say that by demolishing the dams the Germans might create "great destructive waves" that "would destroy everything in the populated industrial valley" of the Roer all the way north into Holland. Thus, once an American force had crossed the Roer, the Germans might flood the river, washing out tactical bridges and exposing the trapped force to defeat in detail.

On the other hand, most intelligence officers and their commanders tended either to dismiss the size and value of any flood that might be produced or to assume that the dams might be knocked out from the air or captured in the natural course of gaining other objectives. The projected role of the V Corps in the new First Army offensive, for example, was to attack from south of the dams across a corner of the Eifel onto the Cologne Plain, thereby, in effect, outflanking the dams and nullifying any importance they might have.

Subsequent events would demonstrate that to be cavalier about the Roer River Dams was both dangerous and expensive. It was also negative and unimaginative, for the dams were a two-edged sword. If the Americans should capture the dams intact, or even if the Germans had to demolish them prematurely, the Germans would be forced either to fall back without a fight behind the Roer or face battle with the possibility of a swollen river at their backs denying supply and reinforcement.

Yet neither the 9th Division nor the V Corps made any

plans for capturing the dams. Indeed, all of October and November would pass before any on the American side would adopt a realistic attitude toward the dams. Until December the First U.S. Army and in later stages the Ninth U.S. Army were to build up along the west bank of the Roer downstream from the dams without making any effort to seize the dams. Yet nobody could cross the Roer until the dams were either captured or destroyed.

Strangely, the Germans, too, were slow to appreciate the full value of the tactical ace they held in the dams. As indicated by the perplexity of Brandenberger and Straube at continued American attacks in the inhospitable Huertgen Forest and by the particular concern of General Schmidt of the *275th Division* for the high ground at Huertgen rather than Schmidt, German commanders in October anticipated no attack on the dams. It would take the cruel events of October and early November to reveal to everyone that Schmidt and its commanding ground was an objective far more vital than first met the eye.

For he who holds Schmidt holds the key to the Roer River Dams.

MUCH TO LEARN IN THE
HUERTGEN FOREST

8 HAD THE Roer River Dams been an objective of the 9th
Division's October attack, it is logical to assume that Collins
or Hodges might have made some extraordinary effort to reinforce the division. As it was, the division commander, General
Craig, was left with his old problem of how to concentrate
sufficient strength to make any real difference between the
new attack and the one-regiment thrust that the 60th Infantry
had launched without success in September.

Even after arrival of the two new divisions to take over a
portion of the V Corps front in the Ardennes–Eifel enabled the
V Corps to shift slightly northward, Craig and his 9th Division
still bore responsibility for nine miles of the line. One regiment,
the 47th Infantry, remained on the defensive at Schevenhuette,
for no one was inclined to give up this deepest penetration
beyond the second band of the Siegfried Line, however illogical it might be to tie up an entire regiment in holding it. Thus
only two regiments were free to attack: the 39th Infantry,
relieved in the Monschau Corridor by corps cavalry, and the
60th Infantry.

Only by entrusting much of the forest to roadblocks
manned by an engineer battalion did General Craig enable
these two regiments to gain a measure of concentration for an
attack. From a line of departure deep within the forest, the

two regiments were to move side by side to cross the Weisser Weh and cut the Lammersdorf–Huertgen highway at the village of Germeter, taking in the process the settlements of Wittscheidt and Richelskaul, which lie north and south, respectively, of Germeter. Taking these settlements would block the only major lateral communications route left to the Germans west of the Roer and at the same time provide egress from the bowels of the forest into the first big clearing along the projected route to Schmidt.

With Wittscheidt and Germeter in hand, the 39th Infantry was to push into the big clearing—a high bald ridge—to take Vossenack, an elongated collection of drab houses and shops stretching almost the full two miles of the ridgeline. From Vossenack the regiment was to cross the imposing gorge of the little Kall River, a stream that rises near Monschau and cuts a deep swath diagonally through the forest before joining the Roer.

Meanwhile, the 60th Infantry, having captured Richelskaul, was to turn back into the depths of the forest to occupy high ground about two forest-cloaked road junctions along the main highway to Lammersdorf, near Deadman's Moor. This would serve both to widen the base of the penetration and to marry it to the puncture of the Siegfried Line near Lammersdorf.

The extent of the 9th Division's objectives in relation to the strength available to achieve them made it plain that either American commanders were gambling or were still discounting German ability to defend the forest. For in the face of anything approaching stanch resistance, two regiments simply were not sufficient to do all the jobs assigned. Once the 39th Infantry turned from Vossenack to Schmidt, for example, the regiment's north flank would extend for six miles, cruelly exposed to counterattack from Huertgen or a dozen other spots. Should a serious counterattack develop, General Craig could provide no reserve other than a battalion of the 60th Infantry holding defensive positions near Jaegerhaus, the woodchopper's hut reached in the September fighting.

Furthermore, if the capture of Schmidt was to be exploited, somebody would have to do an about-face to take from the rear the stubborn pillboxes in the Monschau Corridor. Yet at the same time the 9th Division was obligated to drive north through Huertgen to converge with the main forces of the VII Corps on the edge of the open country at Dueren, ten miles away.

American commanders plainly still engaged in what may be called "breakthrough thinking." They still believed that a major penetration would precipitate German withdrawal at least to the Roer River, and if several penetrations could be achieved, withdrawal all the way to the Rhine. Thus, despite the gloom of the Huertgen Forest, the inherent weakness of the attacking force, and the doubts that might haunt the men down at the foxhole level who knew what was involved in the cruel charge and countercharge in Deadman's Moor, the 9th Division was to attack in an aura of great expectations.

Private First Class Herbert Gripan of the *5th Luftwaffe Fortress Battalion* shared a slit trench with an older man whom he had never seen, of course, until ten days before. The trench was three feet deep, topped with logs covered with soil and with branches from dark green firs. Even though the subofficers allowed Gripan and his companion no fires, the slit trench was dry and fairly warm as long as the two men huddled together and covered themselves with blankets. To supplement each man's issue blanket, they had another taken from a man who was killed and would not need it any more.

Gripan's new friend slept much of the time and the two-hour stints of guard duty in the fighting foxholes near by recurred more often than one might have believed possible, yet the two men still found time to do considerable talking. Gripan had served two years in Russia, his friend three years in Italy and France. Neither had been in the actual front lines before.

Sometimes they talked about what they would do when the *Ami* came. Gripan's companion said he had heard rumors that the Americans shot all prisoners found wearing the Iron Cross, First Class, but neither man believed it. They agreed that capture by the Americans was nothing to fear. Not that they intended to surrender. There was little talk of surrender. Naturally, some said it would be better to be captured and come home after the war with limbs intact, but no one dared talk openly about going over to the enemy. After all, they were fighting now on German soil.

Gripan had no real fear of the American infantry. At least,

others had told him as much, and he saw no reason not to feel the same way. The American infantryman seldom attacked unless his tanks and planes led the way. The tanks and planes were what Gripan feared. Mortar and artillery fire, too, of course. He already had experienced some shelling. It crashed in great thundering salvos in the forest, but as long as you were inside your slit trench with the logs and sod above you, it was more frightening than destructive.

Because Gripan and his companion had been on patrol the night before, they slept late the last morning. Emerging from the slit trench, Gripan made his way to the company command post in a pillbox and returned with two canteens filled with hot coffee. Then they ate a breakfast of bread, margarine, and sardines, saved from their hot meal of the afternoon before. They always had one hot meal during the day, usually in the afternoon. The hour depended on whether American planes and artillery interrupted movement from the rear. Sometimes the food arrived quite late.

They had finished eating breakfast when the platoon sergeant came by to check whether they were still there and whether either man wanted to go on sick call. He brought some mail for Gripan's companion and a copy of the army news sheet, *Mitteilungen für die Truppen*. The news sheet was so full of propaganda nobody would have read it except there was nothing else to read.

Soon it was Gripan's turn to go on guard. Taking over from another man in a foxhole about ten yards away, he stood or knelt in the hole for two hours. Nothing happened. The sector had been quiet for over a week now, with no sign of the enemy. Though artillery shells passed overhead occasionally, almost stirring the tops of the tall firs, they landed far to the rear.

His two hours up, Gripan stopped by the command post in the pillbox to see if the hot food had arrived. The pillbox was dark and murky, lit only by candles. None of the officers was there, only some subofficers and a few runners. Everybody was sitting around on packing cases reading letters or the news sheet and waiting for the telephone to ring.

Gripan took the food—noodle soup, boiled potatoes, fresh pork, and bread (he did not bother with the coffee, since they had some left from breakfast)—and went back to his slit trench. His friend was delighted the food had come so early.

Before night came, Gripan had another uneventful tour of guard duty, and then, in fading light, he found time to write a letter on paper borrowed from a man in another trench. He told his family all was well. What was the point in giving news that might discourage them?

It started to rain after dark, a cold, relentless rain, but it did not bother Gripan and his companion so long as they were in their slit trench. But at eight o'clock the sergeant came. Both men were to go on patrol again.

Gripan swore to himself. Why didn't they pick somebody else for a change?

Five men made up the patrol. Because the word was that the Americans were planning another attack, the patrol was to try to take a prisoner so they might check on the enemy's intentions and his strength.

As the patrol moved out, it was so dark that Gripan could see no more than six paces ahead of him, and then could only make out vague forms. For about an hour they moved cautiously through the woods, not hearing a sound. Then the patrol leader motioned the men to halt. It would be better, the patrol leader said, if they split up, two men going one way, three another. In an hour, he would fire a flare from a signal pistol to indicate they were to reassemble to go back to their positions, bringing prisoners with them if either group had any.

Gripan did not think much of this arrangement. He did not even know what color signal flare the patrol leader intended to fire, but he thought it best not to question. In any event, he saw no flare at all. After wandering about rather aimlessly in the woods, he and his companion decided there was nothing to do but lie down and sleep as best they could right where they were.

The next morning they woke up to find themselves only a few yards from an American tank.

What was a man to do, Gripan asked himself, but surrender?

To infantrymen of the 9th Division, waiting nervously beneath the dark tent of fir branches, the morning of October 5 was long and tense. The question was, Were the low gray clouds too thick for the planes to come? Two groups of P-47 Thunderbolts, more than a hundred planes, were to start the attack on Schmidt by dive-bombing German positions in the woods and at Germeter. But when noon came and the clouds persisted, General Craig postponed the attack. The infantrymen breathed again.

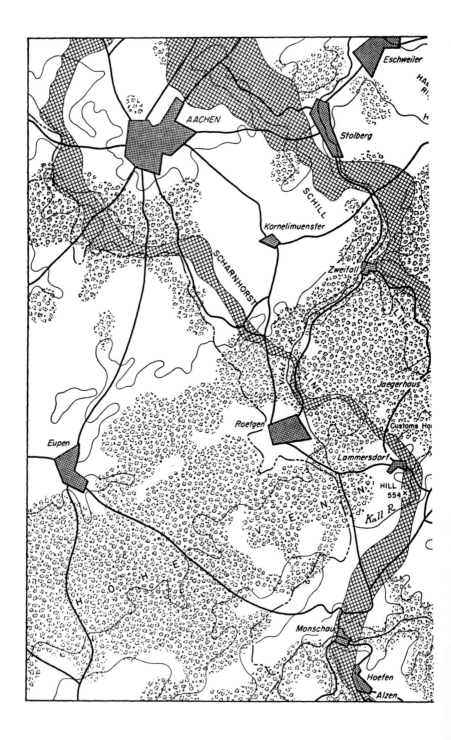

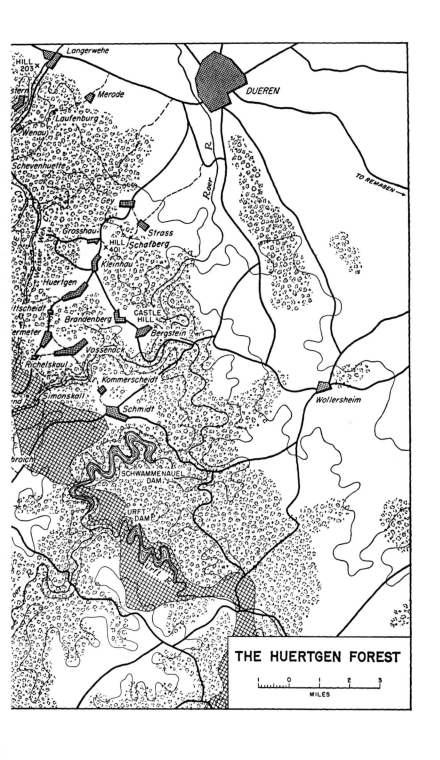

THE HUERTGEN FOREST

0 1 2 3

MILES

The next day it was much the same at first. Though the weather over the forest had cleared, the word was that fog persisted over the airfields in Belgium. To the infantrymen, it had begun to look like another dry run until, at last, shortly after ten o'clock, the heavy sound of plane motors drew near.

Against targets marked with red smoke by the artillery, the bombing began. Diving low, the P-47's struck the wooded eastern slopes of the Weisser Weh valley, the village of Germeter, and the road junctions—the 60th Infantry's objectives —deep in the woods near Deadman's Moor. The explosions were deafening, reverberating in wild, uncontrolled thunder through the forest, but no one could see through the dense trees what damage the bombs did.

As the planes soared away into the distance, outgoing shells from the throats of big artillery pieces whirred, like one rushing freight train after another, across the tops of the fir trees.

Three minutes of fire.

Five minutes of silence.

Two more minutes of fire.

At 11:30, attack.

For men of the 2d Battalion, 60th Infantry, it was only a short walk from an imaginary point in the forest called the line of departure to the first German fire. The men had advanced only a few yards when they ran head on into a pillbox. No one could have known it at the time, but this battalion was destined to fight here for almost a week and to lose most of its men in the process. Thus one-fifth of the 9th Division's assault strength was tied up from the start, not by fire from the enemy's main line but from an outpost position.

On the very first day one company of the 2d Battalion lost all but two of its officers and by nightfall had only sixty men, little more than a platoon. The biggest problem was mortar and artillery fire, for as everybody who entered the Huertgen Forest eventually would come to know, tree bursts more than doubled the effectiveness of shellfire, particularly among attacking infantrymen, whose only protection against the lethal fragments from above was the clothing on their backs. Set with instantaneous fuses, the shells burst on the slightest contact, spraying down metal death. One battalion not even engaged by small-arms fire during the first day lost a hundred men in the shelling.

Almost every move was painfully slow. Paying the severe penalty almost always imposed by inadequate preattack patrolling—a fault shared by many American units at this stage of the war—the men of the 9th Division often got their first indication of enemy positions only when the Germans began to fire. With forward troops pinned to the ground, company or battalion commanders usually sent a maneuvering unit stumbling blindly through the forest around one flank, where, as often as not, this unit too struck stalwart opposition and the whole fire and maneuver process had to be slowly, painfully repeated.

Help from tanks or tank destroyers usually was out of the question. Because only one trail led east through either regimental sector, and because mines and felled trees covered by German machine guns blocked these and the firebreaks, neither tanks nor tank destroyers could get forward. So closely locked were the combatants that the artillery could not range in close enough to have immediate impact on the fighting. The same with fighter-bombers, which roamed the skies whenever the weather permitted. The Germans, on the other hand, fighting from bunkers and log-covered foxholes, were relatively impervious to shelling and could bring their mortars and artillery to bear almost atop their own positions without damage to themselves. For the most part, the combat was reduced to the simple equation of man against man, hand grenade against hand grenade, rifle against rifle, machine gun against machine gun. This way, the usual American advantage in firepower and armament went for nought, and the German advantage of log-covered refuge was telling.

Two exceptions to the pedestrian pace developed, both on the second day, October 7. While a squadron of Thunderbolts bombed and strafed Germeter, a company of the 39th Infantry, maneuvering around a nest of pillboxes on the wooded slope beyond the Weisser Weh, slipped through a hole in the German positions. Unnoticed, the company gained the edge of the woods overlooking Germeter. Though the battalion commander, Colonel Thompson, followed immediately with the rest of his battalion, he hesitated to send his men beyond the concealment of the woods into the village until tanks or antitank guns could get forward and until he could contrive some means of supply other than the long, arduous hand-carry through the woods.

In the 60th Infantry's sector, the veteran woodsmen of Chatfield's battalion faced much the same situation. Committed around a flank of the pillbox that was holding up the 2d Battalion, Chatfield's men as dusk fell were overlooking the settlement of Richelskaul. Like Thompson, Chatfield was reluctant to debouch from the woods without tanks or antitank guns and without some means of vehicular supply.

Word of these two breaks passed like electricity up the chain of command. Both regimental commanders promptly ordered engineers to double their efforts to open either the trails or a firebreak, and the usually unexcitable division commander, General Craig, hurried to the regimental command posts to exhort everybody to press the advantages. But exhortation was one thing, taking out the mines and felled trees under fire and then negotiating the marshy ground with ponderous tanks was another. Not until nightfall on the third day, October 8, were tanks and tank destroyers able to reach the two battalions.

As both Chatfield and Thompson had recognized, a threat to the lateral highway running through Germeter and Richelskaul would bring prompt German reply. Hardly had daylight come on the 8th when General Schmidt sent a reserve battalion of his *275th Division* against Thompson's battalion west of Germeter and another against Chatfield's men near Richelskaul.

Both German forces counterattacked sharply, but this time it was the Germans and not the Americans who were exposed to lethal tree bursts and the confusions of the forest. As American artillery roared, the Germans fell back in disorder, leaving behind a pitiful profusion of dead and wounded.

The three days of renewed fighting in the Huertgen Forest, culminating in the carnage of the two counterattacks, convinced Hans Schmidt that he faced an enemy with an unlimited supply of fresh troops specially trained and experienced in forest fighting. He asked the corps commander, General Straube, for help. Straube in turn telephoned General Brandenberger, but the army commander was less concerned about the threat in the woods than that posed by the attack of the XIX Corps north of Aachen. Brandenberger, fully occupied with seeking reserves to build a dike around the hole in the West Wall, proffered General Schmidt two fortress infantry battalions, which the insatiable forest quickly chewed up.

The counterattacks beaten back and tanks and tank destroyers at last on hand, Chatfield's battalion of the 60th Infantry moved early on October 9 to break out of the woods at Richelskaul. Using a wedge formation with a platoon of Sherman tanks commanded by Staff Sgt. Ralph B. Bertier at the point, the battalion moved so swiftly against Richelskaul that the Germans had no chance to fight back. Blazing cannon and machine guns on the tanks pinned the Germans to their foxholes and cellars, except for a lone lieutenant who dared to rise and fire a *Panzerfaust* at the lead tank. Though the rocket hit the turret of the tank, slightly wounding the tank commander, the crew quickly turned its 75mm. piece on the lieutenant. With one round the big gun ripped the German officer in two.

This so demoralized the other Germans that most of them either surrendered or fled. Nearly a hundred were soon on their way back to prisoner compounds; fifty more were dead. An even dozen *Panzerfausts* lay abandoned, their owners too terrified to fire them after what had happened to their lieutenant.

Within an hour after the attack began, the half a dozen battered buildings that were Richelskaul were in hand. This meant that Lee Chatfield's woodsmen now held a portion of the Lammersdorf–Huertgen highway and might turn south again into the forest toward the two road junctions in an effort to gain control of the highway to Lammersdorf.

The 39th Infantry, meanwhile, had also cut the Lammersdorf–Huertgen highway, not at Gemeter but at Wittscheidt.

As this regiment's reserve battalion came up on the left to protect Colonel Thompson's flank, two platoons just as night fell gained a toehold in the first buildings.

Through the night of the ninth, small-arms fire from adjacent houses and fire from self-propelled guns up the road toward Huertgen constantly harassed these two platoons. Daylight was approaching when the German fire suddenly increased. Before anybody could send help or even call for artillery support, a German company overran the platoons. Retaking the buildings with the aid of tanks was about all that could be accomplished here through October 10. Of the forty-eight men in the two platoons that had entered Wittscheidt, all that was found was the body of one man. The others were captured.

Wary over the fight at Wittscheidt, Colonel Thompson delayed his move into Germeter until his patrols reported German withdrawal, obviously in deference to the American penetrations north and south of the village. After five days of intense fighting, the 39th Infantry at last had captured its first major objective, only a mile beyond its line of departure, at a cost of over 500 casualties.

Again it remained for Chatfield's battalion of the 60th Infantry to make the next big break in the pattern of the fighting. Attacking at noon on October 10, the men moved south from Richelskaul toward a pillbox-studded road junction near a forester's lodge called Raffelsbrand.

The first impression was of dreary repetition of the pedestrian pace that had prevailed most of the time elsewhere in the Huertgen Forest. A driving rain added to the misery, and Sergeant Bertier's tanks soon were frustrated by a mine-infested roadblock.

Then suddenly, as Company A knocked out a pillbox alongside the highway, the drive picked up momentum. Held up again at a second pillbox, Company A's commander, Capt. J. B. Moore, asked Chatfield to let him bypass it. Chatfield radioed approval. Under constant urging from Moore, who had come to believe that the only way to succeed in the forest was to get moving and keep moving, Company A advanced

as fast as the men could walk. Bunches of startled Germans—
more than a hundred men in all—gave themselves up.

With Company B close behind, the men of Company A in
less than three hours after leaving Richelskaul seized what
became known as the Raffelsbrand road junction. Their audacious tactics clearly had taken the Germans by surprise. Unfortunately, Moore and his men failed to go far enough beyond
the road junction itself to discover that they had approached the
rear of a strong position in the second band of Siegfried Line
defenses. Some twelve pillboxes remained undetected. The
men of Chatfield's battalion and many other men who came
into the forest after them would deplore the oversight.

Hoping to duplicate Chatfield's fast thrust, the 60th Infantry commander, Col. John G. Van Houten, on October 11
relinquished the defensive position near Jaegerhaus to a troop
of cavalry and brought forward what was in effect his reserve
battalion. He sent this force to push beyond Raffelsbrand to
the regiment's final objective, the second road junction where
a mud-paved Weisser Weh valley road joined the Lammersdorf–Huertgen highway.

The men of this battalion unfortunately had first to tie up
the loose ends of the previous day's swift gain. Early on October 11 they became fruitlessly embroiled with pillboxes Chatfield's men had bypassed and made no headway toward the
second road junction. Nor could Chatfield provide any help,
for at daylight the Germans began a series of small but potent
counterattacks.

Events on October 11 in the 60th Infantry's sector might
have proven thoroughly discouraging had not the 2d Battalion,
held up for so long by the pillbox in Deadman's Moor, at last
begun to make measured but steady progress against the pillbox and the dug-in enemy around it. The attrition of long days
of fighting at last had begun to tell on the German defenders.
Not for three days, prisoners reported, had the Germans eaten.
When the main pillbox fell, the battalion pushed over 800 yards
to the south to pose a threat to the same road junction that the
reserve battalion had tried in vain to reach.

A threat it was, but not much of a threat, in view of the

impoverished condition of the 2d Battalion—no more than a shell of the unit that had begun to fight in the forest six days earlier. Hardly any of the rifle companies was now anything more than a reinforced platoon, and even this strength depended in large measure on bug-eyed replacements who had begun to arrive in small, frightened driblets.

Like those who entered the forest before them, these replacements had to become accomplished woodsmen almost overnight, or they had no chance to survive. Foxholes, the men soon learned, were almost worthless unless roofed with logs and sod, for seldom did a shell burst on the ground and spray its fragments upward. Death came from the treetops. If you were caught by shelling in the open, it was useless to throw yourself to the ground for protection, for this merely exposed more body surface to the fragments from above. Those who stood or crouched at the base of a tree lived longest. To move about at all at night, more than one old forest hand told a newcomer, was inviting death. In the darkness, too many men shot first, investigated later. Adjusting mortar and artillery fire by sight, forward observers would tell you, was like asking a blind man to read. Adjustment by sound was the only way, and the effect of the trees on sound—at once muffling yet magnifying—made this difficult. For most individuals, getting lost in the forest was strictly a personal problem. "He was our B.A.R.-man," a squad leader would report later. "He set out for the aid station. That was the last we saw of him." It was as simple as that. Nobody left the protection of his own hole to search for you. On the other hand, if you were a squad leader, or a patrol leader, or the man in charge of a supply-carrying party, perhaps somebody might miss you and look for you, because lives depended on you. If you had a map—which was unusual unless you were a platoon leader or a company commander—you might locate yourself in the forest by means of cement survey markers to be found at intersections of firebreaks. Numbers on these corresponded to numbered squares on the maps. Efficient, these Germans. Deadly efficient. But if you had no map, try a compass and head west, always west. That is, if you had a compass.

There was much to learn in the Huertgen Forest.

While the 60th Infantry was re-entering the forest to take the two road junctions, the 39th Infantry at the same time was attempting to move farther into the open, onto the bald ridge crowned by the elongated village of Vossenack. From Vossenack, the regiment was to cross the gorge of the Kall River to Schmidt.

To men of the 39th Infantry who had come to know the forest and its viselike embrace, it was frightening to come into the light. It was like being blind and hating blindness, then gaining sight and hating what you saw. Several times during October 11, men of Colonel Thompson's battalion tried to move across the open ground from Germeter to Vossenack; but each time German assault guns in the distance knocked out the supporting tanks with uncanny accuracy, and without tanks the infantrymen could not brave the machine-gun and mortar fire that lashed the open ground. To many a man, the forest took on an attractiveness heretofore unrealized.

Just how the forest might be turned to advantage quickly became apparent when shortly after midday another battalion passed from Wittscheidt into a wooded draw extending along the northern edge of the Vossenack clearing. Brushing aside a show of resistance at the fringe of the woods, the men continued almost unhindered for over a mile to reach a point opposite the open northeastern nose of the Vossenack Ridge.

The battalion commander, Lt. Col. R. H. Stumpf, was preparing in late afternoon to emerge from the woods onto the ridge, cutting off Vossenack from the rear, when the division commander, General Craig, intervened. Louis Craig, the sane, sober type who preferred to fight on terms laid down by the field manuals but who so far had had little chance to follow them, was cautious. All the Germans would have to do to defeat Stumpf's move against Vossenack, Craig reasoned, was to strike from the north across the tail of the battalion. He ordered Stumpf to delay until the next morning when Thompson's men in Germeter might launch another attack against Vossenack from the west. In the meantime, the 39th Infantry's reserve battalion was to take over at Wittscheidt and build a secure line in the woods west of that settlement to protect the regimental north flank.

The 39th Infantry's north flank had from the first bothered commanders at every level. Joe Collins of the VII Corps, for example, had noted the problem during a visit to the 39th Infantry's command post and had ordered the engineers manning roadblocks west of the Weisser Weh to defend the road-net in the valley itself. This helped, but it still left more than half a wooded mile between the valley and Wittscheidt through which the Germans might strike. A strong counterattack south through the woods might cut off not only Stumpf's battalion, stretched in a long, fingerlike column of companies in the wooded draw north of Vossenack, but also Thompson's battalion at Germeter. Should the thrust reach Richelskaul, the bulk of the 60th Infantry might also be trapped.

As the 39th Infantry's reserve battalion moved into position to defend the flank, prospects were bright for success the next day, October 12. Though no battalion in either of the two regiments could field more than 300 men, so heavy had been the attrition of the forest fighting, the 9th Division obviously had made serious inroads on the German defenses. On the twelfth, the 60th Infantry, was to try again to take the last of its objectives, the road junction at the head of the Weisser Weh valley. Meanwhile, the 39th Infantry was to carry Vossenack, thus genuinely rupturing the enemy's positions and enabling a rapid thrust across the Kall to Schmidt.

If guarded optimism was the attitude on the American side, it would have been logical to assume comparable gloom in the German command. But this was not so. For the day before, on October 10, important visitors in the person of the *Seventh Army* commander, General Brandenberger, and the *74th Corps* commander, General Straube, had come to the *275th Division's* command post. The dangerous American penetration of the West Wall north of Aachen, Brandenberger said, had been contained, and Field Marshal Model at *Army Group B* had promised reserves for that fight. The time was happily at hand when the *Seventh Army* could provide at least a measure of help in the Huertgen Forest.

During the night of October 11, trucks carrying 1,200 men of an *ad hoc* force called *Regiment Wegelein* rolled north from a quiet sector along the Luxembourg border. Commanded by a colonel from whom the unit drew its name, *Regiment Wegelein* had an unusually large complement of machine guns and mortars. The men were young and well trained, with half of them tabbed as candidates for officers' school. *Regiment Wegelein*, Brandenberger ordered, was to attack south through the woods west of Wittscheidt and cut off the American penetrations at Germeter and north of Vossenack. At the same time, Schmidt and his *275th Division* were to muster every available man to attack from the south down the Weisser Weh valley. Together the two thrusts were to cut off both the 39th and 60th Regiments.

Unhappily for the Germans, *Regiment Wegelein* failed to complete its move over winding, blacked-out Eifel roads until well after midnight. The commander, Col. Wolfgang Wegelein, urged General Schmidt to allow him to delay his attack, at least until he could lay telephone lines to assure adequate artillery support. But Schmidt refused. To Schmidt it was obvious that the Americans were poised to take Vossenack. Once they held the Vossenack Ridge, he believed, they would turn north against the roadnet at Huertgen. *Regiment Wegelein* would have to attack at once, Schmidt insisted, or all chance to cut them off would be lost.

The first indication the 39th Infantry had of impending counterattack came at seven o'clock the morning of the twelfth in the form of a brief but sharp artillery preparation. Firing machine guns, burp guns, and rifles, the Germans of *Regiment Wegelein* charged through the early-morning light across a shallow draw that fronted the hastily organized positions west of Wittscheidt. In a matter of minutes, the first wave poured through an overextended American line and surged across the trail leading into Germeter, the lifeline of Thompson's 1st Battalion. Though Thompson hurriedly turned two of his companies against the penetration, the depleted units were too weak to force the Germans back.

The regimental commander, Colonel Bond, had no reserve to call on. Nor could the division commander, General Craig, do much to help. Before hurrying forward to Bond's command post, Craig alerted two companies of the 47th Infantry at Schevenhuette to be ready to move if needed, but it would be some time before these companies could get into position to influence the action.

For Bond and Craig it was difficult to piece together any coherent picture of the fight from the fragments of information that filtered back to them. Assuming that Stumpf's battalion north of Vossenack was also under attack, Bond ordered Stumpf to disengage and fall back on Wittscheidt, there to turn and strike the Germans in the woods in flank. This Colonel Stumpf set out to do, but it would be daylight the next morning before he could attack. About all there was left for either Bond or Craig was to urge the division artillery on to greater efforts in pounding the woods whence the Germans came.

Unknown to the Americans, all was far from right on the German side. Colonel Wegelein's communications, which he had protested before the attack, had failed utterly, so that he himself knew as little about what was taking place as did Bond and Craig. What was more, Wegelein was left with no way to control his artillery. Though his troops had penetrated the American positions, they had not eliminated them, for here and there American groups held out in stubborn little pockets of resistance.

Nor did the timing or strength of the *275th Division's* complementary attack from the south do much to help. General Schmidt had managed to assemble a force totaling no more than 300 men, and these failed to move until late in the morning, after much of the impact of Wegelein's strike had begun to wear off. The complementary thrust accomplished little more than to prevent the 60th Infantry from renewing its push toward the road junction at the head of the Weisser Weh.

Night passed in the Huertgen Forest with confusion reigning on both sides. Firing at various points erupted spasmodically as men of one force or the other bumped into an adversary or imagined they did. Meanwhile, General Schmidt ordered Colonel Wegelein to renew the counterattack the next morning, but this became impossible when an order arrived that all officer candidates in *Regiment Wegelein* were to be withdrawn. This cut Wegelein's strength in half and took away his most effective fighters. In exchange for some 500 casualties on the first day, *Regiment Wegelein* had gained only a tenuous hold on the supply trail into Germeter.

By mid-afternoon on October 13, Colonel Bond had sufficient control over his regiment to begin the job of eliminating the German penetration. It nevertheless took three days for the 39th Infantry to restore the original flank position and mop up all the Germans in the woods. In light of the depleted condition of *Regiment Wegelein*, this was testimony less to stout opposition than to the fact that the 39th Infantry was spent and groggy. One company, for example, had but two platoons left, one with twelve men, another with thirteen. The regiment plainly was too weak to renew the attack on Vossenack, much less continue on to Schmidt.

The German commander, Colonel Wegelein, himself became a casualty in the closing days of the engagement. As he was walking, alone and unarmed, not far from his foxhole, a sergeant from Company E shot him. On his body were maps and detailed plans for *Regiment Wegelein's* counterattack.

For a German officer who had served efficiently since 1921, this parading alone and unarmed through the forest close to American lines was strange behavior. Had Wegelein become so disillusioned with the failure and destruction of his unit that he had courted death?

Or was it that Wegelein, like so many others in the thick forest, had simply lost his way?

For several days after the German counterattacks, first one unit of the 60th Infantry, then another, tried again and again to take the regiment's last assigned objective, the road junction at the head of the Weisser Weh. But these were feeble efforts and had no chance of success until General Craig brought in from Schevenhuette the two companies of the 47th Infantry which earlier he had alerted to form a division reserve.

By October 16, eleven days after the two regiments of the 9th Division had begun to attack in the Huertgen Forest, the road junction was in hand, but this was unquestionably as far as the 9th Division could go. Falling far short of Schmidt, the division had penetrated some 3,000 yards into the forest, but in the process had paid dearly with more than one casualty per yard. The two regiments and attached troops had lost 4,500 men killed, wounded, and missing, a body blow that could not be set right simply by sending in individual replacements, no matter how courageous. The Germans for their part had lost 1,300 men captured and an estimated 2,000 killed or wounded.

The outcome of the 9th Division's attack meant that the precondition for a new First Army drive—a secure flank in the Huertgen Forest—could not be met. This realization came at a time when troops of the XIX Corps north of Aachen and of the 1st Division in the city were encountering resolute defenders who exacted heavy tribute for each small gain. General Hodges' optimistic plans of late September for a bold push to the Roer and then to the Rhine thus foundered in a series of preliminary engagements that failed to develop as planned. The projected supporting attack by General Gerow's V Corps northeast across a corner of the Eifel above the Roer Dams had to be canceled.

The First Army—indeed, the Allied armies as a whole—had to come up with something new, something big, if they were to gain the Rhine.

WHAT TO DO ABOUT THE HUERTGEN FOREST?

9   A PLAN for something new, something big, was the next order of business for the Allied high command. Meeting at Brussels on October 18, the Supreme Commander, General Eisenhower, and his army group commanders, Montgomery and Bradley, pondered a new course.

The big problem, even this late in October, still was supply. Though Antwerp had been taken, the German hold on the banks of the Schelde Estuary continued to deny use of the city as a port. Until these banks could be freed, Antwerp was a jewel that could not be worn for want of a setting. On the other hand, since Eisenhower had already directed Field Marshal Montgomery to proceed with this task, an early end to the logistical problems appeared likely.

In all planning both before and after the Normandy invasion, General Eisenhower had subscribed to a strategy of advancing on a broad front and building up along the Rhine River before launching final thrusts into the heart of Germany. Though he had deviated slightly from this approach in September, when he had strengthened Montgomery's 21st Army Group by sending the First U.S. Army north of the Ardennes, this had been designed to gain immediate objectives like Antwerp. The plans worked out at Brussels marked a full return to the so-called "broad front strategy."

Eisenhower directed Bradley's 12th Army Group, and specifically Hodges' First Army, to make the main effort. Attacking early in November, the First Army was to cross the Rhine south of Cologne. A new force, the Ninth U.S. Army under Lt. Gen. William H. Simpson, was to protect the First Army's north flank while Patton's Third Army in Lorraine advanced along the south flank.

General Bradley's plan, in turn, involved several shifts of command. Hodges' First Army was to relinquish the XIX Corps to the Ninth Army. Hodges in exchange was to receive the VIII Corps and a new division for Joe Collins' VII Corps.

On October 21, the same day that General Hodges received his instructions, Aachen fell. With a new corps to handle the defensive assignment in the Ardennes–Eifel and relieved of responsibility for Aachen and the XIX Corps sector north of Aachen, Hodges could gain genuine concentration for renewing the attack to the Rhine. To Hodges, the VII Corps still looked like the logical choice for the main effort. Only one big problem still remained:

What to do about the Huertgen Forest?

Convinced that the forest had to be taken, Hodges apparently gave no serious thought to bypassing it. This he might have accomplished by sending the V Corps south of the Roer Dams to outflank the forest. He might have pushed to open country beyond Schevenhuette, then south along the Roer to cut in behind the forest. Or he might have attacked to take the Roer Dams, which in American hands could have been used like some superweapon to force the Germans to retire behind the Roer.

Instead, Hodges continued to think in terms of sweeping the forest and gaining a secure right flank along the headwaters of the Roer. Thus, in Hodges' mind, all the reasons earlier advanced for sending the 9th Division to Schmidt remained as valid as before.

Somebody had to take Schmidt.

Lest the main effort be weakened by leaving responsibility for Schmidt with the VII Corps, Hodges transferred the objective to Gerow's V Corps. Hoping to assist the main effort further by luring enemy strength away from it, Hodges told General Gerow to attack, if weather permitted, on the first day of November, and regardless of weather, no later than the second. He also directed Gerow to seize the woods line overlooking Huertgen so that a division of the VII Corps later might use it as a point of departure.

With the 9th Division in dire straits in the Huertgen Forest, Gerow turned to a Pennsylvania National Guard unit, veteran of heavy fighting in Normandy, the 28th Infantry Division. As part of the V Corps, the 28th had participated in the early attempt to pierce the Siegfried Line in the Ardennes–Eifel, but since then had been resting in relative quiet below Monschau.

After taking Schmidt, the 28th Division was to come in on the rear of the Monschau Corridor, much as the 9th Division had been scheduled to do. Though intent on husbanding the bulk of the V Corps for later attack south of the Roer Dams, Gerow nevertheless ordered a combat command of the 5th Armored Division to prepare to attack frontally against the face of the corridor as the 28th Division came in from the rear. Gerow also reinforced the 28th Division strongly. In addition to the normal attachments of a battalion each of medium tanks and self-propelled tank destroyers, he gave the division a battalion of towed tank destroyers, a chemical mortar battalion,* a detachment of forty-seven "weasels" (little jeep-sized tracked cargo carriers for cross-country movement), and the entire 1171st Engineer Combat Group of three engineer battalions. In direct and general support he placed eight battalions and a separate battery of corps artillery.

Resembling the earlier plan for the 9th Division, that for the 28th Division failed to avoid some of the dangers inherent in the previous plan. Impressed—perhaps unduly—by the counterattack the late Wolfgang Wegelein had thrown against the 39th Infantry's flank, General Gerow specified that the 28th Division use an entire regiment for the task of gaining the woods line overlooking Huertgen. Aware that the division

---

* Such battalions were equipped with 4.2-inch mortars designed for firing chemical shells but highly effective firing smoke, white phosphorus, or high explosives.

would require a direct line of supply into the Monschau Corridor once Schmidt had fallen, Gerow specified further that another regiment open secondary roads leading into the corridor in the woods below Richelskaul. This left the 28th Division with only one regiment for making the main thrust to Schmidt, the same situation faced by the 9th Division, with the same problem of an elongated north flank.

This failed to disturb the First Army commander, General Hodges. He considered the plan "excellent." He particularly liked the possibility that the thrust to secure the woods line overlooking Huertgen might appear to the enemy to be the main effort. Visiting the 28th Division's command post, Hodges came away impressed. He found the division "in fine fettle, rarin' to go, and optimistic over giving the Boche a fine drubbing."

That Courtney Hodges gained this impression meant that something was wrong somewhere at the start, for the 28th Division commander, Maj. Gen. Norman D. Cota, was decidedly unhappy with the attack plan. Cota felt keenly that the dictates imposed in part by army, in part by corps, left him with little initiative.

A big, ruddy-faced New Englander whose friends called him "Dutch," Cota while an assistant division commander in Normandy had gained a reputation for personal daring and courage. Not one to shirk an assignment, no matter what its danger, he nevertheless disliked the job of taking Schmidt. Moving in with his men to relieve the 9th Division, he found himself and his troops in a dismal forest. All about them lay emergency rations containers, artillery-stripped trees, stacks of unearthed mines along muddy, almost impassable firebreaks and trails, shell and mine craters by the hundreds, pitiful remains of deer cut down by artillery and mines, and men from graves registration units still removing the bloated bodies of the fallen. The 9th Division troops were dirty, unshaven, nervous, morose. Everywhere the forest frowned—wet, cold, miserable, hostile.

Cota's problem was how best to use the limited freedom left him to overcome the immense difficulties imposed by the divergent missions and by the harshly assertive nature of the terrain. The Roer and subsidiary stream lines, including the Kall River, slice the sector into three sharply defined ridges, all of them bald but wreathed on every side by dense forest. Cota's attack obviously had to move first to the Germeter–Vossenack Ridge in the center. Since Cota had no force available to take the ridge on the left, the Brandenberg–Bergstein Ridge, he would have to operate under enemy guns blasting from that ridge with no help except from artillery firing with limited ammunition allotments. Since the third ridge, crowned by the objective of Schmidt, is higher than the Germeter–Vossenack Ridge, Cota's troops would have to fight an uphill battle all the way to Schmidt.

The roads—such as they were—ran along the bald high ground. A dirt road linked Germeter and Vossenack. From Vossenack, the map showed a narrow cart track dropping precipitously to the Kall River, then rising tortuously to Kommerscheidt and Schmidt. The existence of this track could not be verified from aerial photographs and had not been confirmed by patrols, yet the 28th Division would have to chance its being there, for no other route existed for supplying the troops who would go to Kommerscheidt and Schmidt. Through Schmidt runs the main highway leading from the Monschau Corridor, the principal supply route for the enemy's *89th Division*. Another highway leads downhill from Schmidt to the Schwammenauel Dam.

Because of the treacherous cart track across the Kall, nobody could guarantee that tanks, tank destroyers, or even towed guns could cross the river. The enemy, on the other hand, might bring in armor over two main highways leading into Schmidt. Cota could only hope that his attached engineers could open the cart track to tanks and that fighter-bombers could prevent German armor from reaching Schmidt. Yet isolating a battlefield of this size was an incredibly difficult assignment for fighter-bombers, provided the November weather even permitted them to operate.

The enemy, of course, looked to be the same grab-bag assortment under General Schmidt's *275th Division* that had op-

posed the 9th Division, but somehow this conglomerate force
had managed to make trouble enough for the 9th. Not to mention the fact that by moving before the general Allied offensive,
the 28th Division would be making the only attack along some
170 miles of front, an engraved invitation to German reserves to
intervene.

The Germans, for their part, quickly established the arrival
of this fresh American division but assumed erroneously that
the American objective was not Schmidt but Huertgen. Thus
they proceeded with a plan to relieve the *89th Division* in the
Monschau Corridor; the *89th* was then to be reorganized for
use in a daring, imaginative plan that Hitler himself had con-
ceived.

Though Hitler still had not made his thinking known to
German commanders below army level, he intended to launch
a grand counteroffensive in December. It was to be staged a
few miles south of Schmidt from the Eifel into the Ardennes.
Like the Americans, the Germans still had not appreciated the
full value of the Roer River Dams; but those at higher levels
who knew of Hitler's plan recognized that they dared not relinquish Schmidt and the high ground around it, which were
vital for maintaining a secure north flank for the counteroffensive.

As determined by General Cota, the 28th Division's attack
was to begin with a preliminary thrust along the Germeter–
Huertgen highway to the woods line overlooking Huertgen.
At the same time, an infantry battalion with the help of tanks
was to clear the Vossenack Ridge. Beginning at noon, the 112th
Infantry was to make the main attack from Richelskaul through
a wooded draw south of the Vossenack Ridge, across the Kall
River, through Kommerscheidt, to Schmidt. A third regiment
was to attack in the woods below Richelskaul while holding out
one battalion to provide a nominal division reserve.

Except for assigning a company of tanks for Vossenack,
General Cota bowed to the difficulties of the terrain and assigned the rest of the tanks and the self-propelled tank destroyers to augment division artillery. Granted all the problems of
vehicular movement through the woods, to use this tactic was

to ignore the experience of the 9th Division. In few cases had the 9th Division made marked progress without tanks or some form of close fire support.

Cota assigned two battalions of the engineers to work on supply trails in the forest, another to improve the cart track across the Kall gorge. Cota charged the latter group specifically with providing security for the Kall trail. Because no American infantry would be in a position to block the gorge, the engineers would be the only force to prevent the Germans from cutting the trail and isolating the troops in Kommerscheidt and Schmidt. Yet when the engineers interpreted Cota's order to mean providing only local security—that is, security for the engineer work force—nobody, Cota included, disputed the interpretation. This showed a surprising lack of appreciation for what the little cart track across the Kall gorge meant in terms of success or failure of the 28th Division's attack.

When the target date of November 1 arrived, rain, fog, and mist forced postponement of the assault. With that kind of weather, there would be no hope of isolating the Schmidt battlefield with fighter aircraft, yet by the terms of General Hodges' original directive, the attack had to be made the next day, regardless of the weather. Predicated on the hope that the 28th Division might divert German reserves from the main drive by the VII Corps, this stipulation on November 1 ceased to have any validity. On that day the army group commander, General Bradley, agreed to postpone the main attack. Because new divisions scheduled to augment the drive had been slow in arriving, Bradley moved the target date back from the fifth of November to the tenth. Even this date was highly tentative, since to insure a big air bombardment, D day had to have fair weather. Bradley specified that the main attack begin on November 10, or the first fair day thereafter, but, in any event, not later than November 16.

Under these terms, a two-week time difference conceivably might develop between the 28th Division's attack and the main attack. Yet nobody seems to have remarked that if the 28th Division jumped off on November 2, and the main drive failed to go until the sixteenth, enemy reserves might chew the

28th Division to pieces and still be free to oppose the main effort. Hodges made no move either to alter the 28th Division's deadline date or to arrange for help should the 28th Division run into trouble.

Nobody intended it, but the 28th Division was, in effect, to be thrown to the wolves.

THE 28TH DIVISION AT SCHMIDT

10 NOVEMBER 2 dawned cold and misty.

A 12,000-round artillery preparation—sizable for a one-division attack—began at eight o'clock, an hour before the infantry was scheduled to move; but not until mid-afternoon were any fighter aircraft able to operate. Even then most planes failed to locate assigned targets, roaming instead far afield in search of other targets. Probably the most notable air action of the day was a mistaken bombing of an American artillery position that killed seven men and wounded seventeen.

At nine o'clock, men of two battalions of the 109th Infantry rose from foxholes and slit trenches and headed north on either side of the Germeter–Huertgen highway. Harassed as much by problems of maintaining direction and contact between units in the thick forest as by German fire, the battalion west of the highway moved with surprising ease. By early afternoon the men were digging in at the woods line overlooking Huertgen. But the other battalion almost at the start ran into a dense antipersonnel minefield a stone's throw from Wittscheidt. Every effort to find a path through the field brought only more cries for "Medic!" Every time engineers tried to clear the mines, machine guns and mortars drove them to cover.

The next day, November 3, the battalion east of the road

was seeking to flank the minefield when some 200 Germans struck the battalion at the woods line. Though noisy, the counterattack posed no real threat, but this the battalion east of the road could not know. Confused by a garbled radio message, the battalion commander, following the age-old maxim to march to the sound of the cannon, sent two companies toward the noise of the counterattack. As these companies became hopelessly enmeshed in the other battalion's fight, the day's attempt to outflank the minefield and take the other half of the 109th Infantry's objective came to an end.

Though the 109th Infantry still had a reserve battalion, attempts to thwart German infiltration behind the advance battalions already had tied up this force. By evening of the second day, November 3, the mold of the 109th Infantry's position had almost set. The regiment had forged a narrow, mile-deep salient into the forest between the Weisser Weh Creek and the Germeter–Huertgen highway. The Germans nevertheless continued to hold the network of trails in the creek bed in a comparable countersalient into American lines. For the next few days, while the men dug deep and roofed their foxholes with logs, the 109th Infantry tried both to eliminate the countersalient and to take the other half of the objective east of the highway. To no avail. Every movement merely increased already alarming casualties and enmeshed the companies and platoons more inextricably in the coils of the forest.

In the meantime, at the same hour on November 2 that the 109th Infantry had moved northward, the 2d Battalion, 112th Infantry, under Lt. Col. Theodore S. Hatzfeld, had attacked with a company of tanks from Germeter to clear the Vossenack Ridge. Assault guns firing from the Brandenberg–Bergstein Ridge knocked out several tanks, but the spinelike village of Vossenack was in hand by early afternoon. As the tanks sought cover among the damaged buildings, the infantry began to dig in on the exposed northeastern nose of the ridge.

Uncomfortably aware that the enemy was watching from the Brandenberg–Bergstein Ridge, more than one man questioned why they had to defend from the open ground when they might accomplish the same thing from concealed positions in the fringe of the village. The only answer was that some planning officer poring over a map had drawn a "goose egg" with a grease pencil over the nose of the ridge. The stroke of the pencil became law. Here the men were to go; here the men were to stay. It was as rudimentary and as obtuse as that.

The 28th Division's main effort began at noon with an attack by the rest of the 112th Infantry under Lt. Col. Carl L. Peterson, a slender, wiry man with reddish-blonde hair and moustache who had grown up in Pennsylvania among the miners, oil-field workers, and tradesmen who even now constituted the hard core of the National Guard regiment's noncommissioned officers. The regiment began to move from Richelskaul to pass through the woods south of Vossenack to take Schmidt.

From the first this was an inauspicious attack altogether unworthy of being called the "main effort." Hardly had the leading battalion begun to move when the first company came under intense small-arms fire. Apparently impressed with the relative ease with which Hatzfeld's 2d Battalion had gained Vossenack, Colonel Peterson committed no more of his regiment, called for only a few volleys of artillery fire, and made no call at all for tanks. Peterson plainly wanted to wait until the next day and move on Schmidt by way of Vossenack, a move that set back by at least half a day the time when Schmidt might be taken.

The division's third regiment, the 110th Infantry, meanwhile had begun what would prove to be a frustrating campaign during which no one apparently recognized that the men had to have direct-fire support or fail. Two battalions attacked at noon on the second, one to take the pillboxes below the Raffelsbrand road junction, the other to push through the woods to a little settlement alongside the Kall River called Simonskall. Seizing these two objectives was the first step toward opening secondary roads into the Monschau Corridor.

Already the forest here had begun to look like a battlefield designed by the Archfiend himself. Shelling had made a debris-littered jungle of the forest floor and cut naked yellow gashes on the trunks of the trees. Here opposing lines were within hand-grenade range, the Germans waiting behind thick entanglements of concertina barbed wire, alive with trip wires, mines, and booby traps. Log-covered bunkers and foxholes almost flush with the ground augmented the pillboxes. Over it all hung a dim, macabre light filtered by dripping branches of dark green firs.

No sooner had the attacking troops risen from their foxholes than a rain of machine-gun and mortar fire brought them to earth. Though men of one battalion worked their way slowly, painfully up to the triple band of concertinas surrounding the pillboxes, they could go no farther. In mid-afternoon, the battalion reeled back, dazed and stricken, to the line of departure. It was much the same with the other battalion. Squads and platoons got lost; mortar shells landing among assault teams carrying explosive charges set off the explosives and blew up the men; an unfailing chatter of machine guns ripped through the trees whenever anybody moved. One man, a replacement, sobbing hysterically, tried to dig himself a hole in the ground with his fingers. In late afternoon, this battalion too staggered back to the line of departure.

These men obviously needed help from tanks or some other direct-fire weapon if they were to succeed. But again on the second day, November 3, nobody made any effort to get tanks or tank destroyers forward. The grave, dedicated, what-choice-did-they-have infantrymen got up again from their holes whenever the noncoms and the lieutenants told them to. With no supporting fire in back of them, they were quickly cut down by the Germans. The story at day's end was all too familiar. In one company, only forty-two men made it back to the line of departure.

As night came on the second day, neither the regimental commander nor General Cota made any effort to send tanks down the muddy, mine-infested firebreaks and trails toward Raffelsbrand. Cota came up with another possible solution. He called upon the 110th Infantry's remaining battalion, the one he had earmarked as a division reserve, to move to Vossenack, then before daylight the next morning to go south through the woods to Simonskall, thereby cutting in behind the entrenched Germans who were thwarting the rest of the regiment.

It was a clever idea in theory and would prove as clever in execution. Yet it nevertheless meant expending the 28th Division's only reserve very early in the operation.

Frustration, even futility, thus reigned on November 3 on both wings of the 28th Division's attack. Not so in the center. Here excitement, elation took over.

The 112th Infantry did it. Passing through Vossenack, two battalions headed southeast into the Kall gorge. Not a bullet, not a shell came from the Germans. Fording the cold, swift-flowing little Kall River, the men picked a way up the steep slope beyond. Pausing in Kommerscheidt only long enough to rout a handful of German service troops, the lead battalion under Lt. Col. Albert M. Flood hurried on to Schmidt. The men got to Schmidt soon after midday, there to meet their first opposition. The darkness that comes early in northern Europe at this time of year had fallen before the last of the German snipers could be mopped up and defensive positions for the night established, but, incredible as it might seem, troops of the 28th Division had captured Schmidt.

One of the largest of the Huertgen Forest settlements, Schmidt sprawls along four roads that intersect in the center of the village. Defending it with only one infantry battalion was a question more of outposts than of a solid line. Though Carl Peterson, the regimental commander, had intended his remaining battalion under Maj. Robert T. Hazlett to share the defense of Schmidt, he decided early in the afternoon to stop Hazlett's men in Kommerscheidt. Like everyone else who had studied the 28th Division's attack plan carefully, Peterson was immensely concerned that his troops in Schmidt might be cut off by a German strike against Kommerscheidt or at some other point between Vossenack and Schmidt.

As night fell, the men preparing to defend Schmidt were cold and wet from fording the Kall, tired from their two-day exertion, and lulled by the ease of their day's conquest. It was far simpler to set up defenses inside the warm, dry houses than to dig foxholes in the cold, wet earth outside. Even in those squads where persistent, unpopular sergeants forced the men to outside positions, few of the men dug deep.

Not until midnight, when sixty antitank mines arrived, was there any form of antitank protection other than the men's bazookas. The mines were brought in by a supply train of three little weasels that had inched across the precipitous Kall trail, and were placed on the three hard-surfaced roads leading into Schmidt, but no effort was made either to dig them in or to camouflage them.

Nor did anybody bother to send out patrols to try to find out if the enemy was near.

The battalion commander, Colonel Flood, was not even in the village himself, having located his command post in a pillbox along the road to Kommerscheidt. The battalion's medical-aid station was even farther to the rear, occupying a log-walled dugout far back in the Kall gorge.

Taking Schmidt had been easy . . . too easy.

With Schmidt in hand and the weather continuing to deny the continuous air cover that would have kept enemy tanks away from Schmidt, the focus of the 28th Division's operations inevitably turned to the cart track across the Kall gorge. On the use that could be made of this narrow path might well rest the fate of the American troops beyond the Kall and the eventual success or failure of the 28th Division's attack.

That this might be the case was hardly apparent from American actions through most of the day of November 3. Word in Vossenack had it that the bridge over the Kall had been demolished, but not until late afternoon did anybody move to check the report. Two officers of the 20th Engineer Battalion, attached to the 112th Infantry for the express purpose of opening the trail and keeping it open, finally reconnoitered the trail in late afternoon. At one point, they reported, the trail was a narrow shelf, one side marked by a sharp rise studded with rock outcroppings, the other by a sheer drop. Yet the trail could be used, the engineers believed, even by tanks. At the Kall River itself, a stone bridge was in good condition.

In gathering darkness, a medium tank company commanded by Capt. Bruce M. Hostrup left Vossenack to cross the gorge, Hostrup himself in the lead. Yet hardly had Hostrup's tank inched more than a quarter of the way from the woods line to the bottom of the gorge than the left shoulder of the trail began to give way. Unable to move farther to the right because of the rock outcroppings in the precipice, Hostrup and his tank almost plunged into the abyss to the left. Gunning his motor in reverse, he backed out, convinced that tanks could not use the trail in its present condition.

When Hostrup reported this development to his battalion commander, word came back that engineers were to work on the trail through the night. Hostrup and his tanks were to be ready to move to Schmidt just before dawn.

Engineers did work on the trail during the night, but they made an incredibly small outlay in men and equipment in light of the importance of the task. Only two platoons worked west of the Kall, and one to the east. None of them had anything more than hand tools at first. Though a bulldozer reached the trail about 2 A.M., it soon broke a cable and was useless. The only vehicles to cross the Kall were the three weasels carrying antitank mines to Schmidt.

Yet for all the failure to get tanks across the Kall, the map in the 28th Division's command post the night of November 3 reflected a surprising number of accomplishments. While the 109th Infantry had gained only half its objective at the woods line overlooking Huertgen, the regiment was well placed to thwart counterattack from the direction of Huertgen. By committing the reserve battalion of the 110th Infantry before daylight to seize Simonskall, General Cota might break the terrible stalemate in the woods around Raffelsbrand. The enemy had produced no surprises, and no German tanks had appeared. Most encouraging of all, the 28th Division had two battalions beyond the Kall, one of them astride the division objective of Schmidt.

Division and corps commanders all along the front began to telephone their congratulations. For all the reservations about the attack, "Dutch" Cota began to feel like—in his own words—"a little Napoleon."

Had Cota and his staff considered two facts about the enemy, no one in the 28th Division could have slept that night. First, during the day, a *volksgrenadier* division had begun relieving the *89th Infantry Division* in the Monschau Corridor. Only minutes before Colonel Flood's men of the 112th Infantry entered Schmidt, two German battalions moving back from the front had passed through the village. They stopped for the night less than a mile beyond Schmidt. A third battalion, nearing Schmidt after midnight, had found its route of withdrawal cut. This battalion dug in astride the road west of Schmidt. Even though Colonel Flood's men did no patrolling during the night, the 28th Division should have known of the *89th Division's* relief; for other units of the V Corps had taken prisoners who revealed the story, and corps intelligence had passed the reports to the 28th Division during the day.

The second fact about the enemy the 28th Division could not have known. The preceding day, November 2, at almost the same moment the 28th Division had begun to attack, staff officers and commanders of *Army Group B*, the *Seventh Army*, and several corps and divisions, including Straube's *74th Corps*, had sat down in a castle near Cologne to play a war game. Conducted by Field Marshal Model, the steadfast, bemonocled *Army Group B* commander, the game was based on a theoretical American attack near Huertgen. Hardly had the play opened when a telephone call came from the *74th Corps* telling of the American thrust and begging reinforcements.

Model promptly directed Erich Straube, the *74th Corps* commander, to get back to his headquarters. Then he went on with the game, this time using actual reports from the front for the play. When news arrived that Vossenack had fallen, Model decided to send to Straube's assistance a small infantry task force from the *116th Panzer Division*. This was Gerhard von Schwerin's old command, now refitted and reorganized under a new commander, Generalmajor Siegfried von Waldenburg, a young, energetic officer specifically chosen to succeed Schwerin because he was tactful and adroit in dealing with subordinates. It was this small infantry force that counterattacked the 109th Infantry with no success at the woods line near Huertgen the morning of the third.

When the map exercise reconvened on the third, news of the failure of the counterattack prompted Model to send an entire panzer grenadier regiment of the *116th Panzer Division* to Huertgen immediately, the rest of the division to follow that night and the next. Since the pattern of American attack gave some indication that Schmidt might also be an objective, Model ordered the units of the *89th Division* already relieved from the Monschau Corridor to halt in place, ready to counterattack, if necessary, at Schmidt.

The *Seventh Army* commander, the indefatigable Erich Brandenberger, had returned from the map exercise to his headquarters soon after nightfall on the third when word came about Schmidt. Brandenberger promptly ordered Waldenburg, the new *116th Panzer Division* commander, to reroute his panzer regiment from Huertgen to Schmidt. While the division's two panzer grenadier regiments were attacking from Huertgen *à la Regiment Wegelein*, some thirty tanks of the panzer regiment were to help the *89th Division* retake Schmidt and Kommerscheidt. The counterattacks were to begin at dawn the next morning, November 4.

On the American side, as daylight approached on the fourth, General Cota was committing his only infantry reserve, a battalion of the 110th Infantry, to push from Vossenack to Simonskall. Little more than an hour after daylight the battalion entered the hamlet alongside the Kall west of Raffelsbrand; but the gain failed to have any effect on the resistance in the pillboxes at Raffelsbrand.

Also, in early-morning darkness on the fourth, crewmen of Captain Hostrup's tanks warmed their motors for another try at crossing the Kall gorge. The lead tank, commanded by 1st Lt. Raymond E. Fleig, almost immediately struck a mine. The explosion ripped a track. The tank partially blocked the trail.

Using a winch, the tankers finally got four tanks past Fleig's disabled vehicle. Fleig himself then mounted the lead tank and by painstaking backing and turning finally reached

the Kall to begin the last lap to Kommerscheidt at daybreak;
but behind him Fleig left the shoulder of the trail at the narrow
spot where passage was made difficult by rock outcroppings
torn and crumbling. The three other tanks nevertheless managed to get to the bottom of the gorge, where one tank stuck
in mud and threw a track.

Captain Hostrup, meanwhile, was trying to get the rest
of his tanks past Fleig's mine-damaged vehicle. The first to try
plunged off the trail, but it came to rest in a position where it
could be used as a buffer for other tanks to pass. Two tanks
made it, but as they neared the rock outcroppings, both slipped
off the trail and threw their tracks.

As daylight came, only three tanks were on their way
beyond the Kall. Behind them, blocking the vital Kall trail,
were five disabled tanks. Not even the dexterous little weasels
could slip through.

The German artillery barrage against Schmidt began just
as an overcast day was breaking. Up and down the elongated
arms of the village the shells ranged. The bombardment
quickly cut American telephone lines, and at this hour sleepy
operators far to the rear failed for a long time to spot the
break and turn on their radios. Thus American artillery was
slow to fight back. Not until an hour and a quarter after the
first German shells fell was the first American artillery concentration fired. It was too late. Already German infantrymen
were streaming toward the village from two sides. From the
northeast, whence came the *116th Panzer Division*, Mark IV
and big Mark V Panther tanks charged with the infantry.

The tanks were unstoppable. Clanking methodically on-
ward in apparent disdain for the antitank mines laid like so
many checker pieces on the hard-surfaced road, they shot up
the landscape. From the buildings, bazookamen frantically
but vainly opened fire on them. At least one bazooka scored a
hit, but for all the effect the rocket had, it might have been
a ping-pong ball. This demoralized the men who saw it.

Confusion mounted. Someone said the word was to withdraw. Someone else passed the word along. Like an insidious
virus the confusion ate into the men and spread from squad

to squad, platoon to platoon, company to company. The battalion commander in his command post in a pillbox along the road to Kommerscheidt was in no position to exert any personal influence to stem the spread of the rumor. Grabbing at rifles and equipment, the men began to race toward Kommerscheidt and into the woods to the southwest.

It was a *sauve qui peut.*

In less than three hours, it was over at Schmidt. Courageous aid men stayed with the wounded. The dead lay unattended.

As the skies cleared around noon, a squadron of P-47's dive-bombed the village, an acknowledgment that the attempt to isolate the Schmidt battlefield from the air had failed.

DEBACLE AT VOSSENACK
AND KOMMERSCHEIDT

11

FROM THE MOMENT the tanks of the *116th Panzer Division* hit Colonel Flood's battalion in Schmidt, the fortunes of the 28th Division began to go rapidly downhill. From time to time efforts to raise them would give every indication of success, yet almost inevitably the downhill course would in the end prevail. In some ways, this was the story of the entire battle of the Huertgen Forest. A push here, a push there, a push anywhere in the right direction might have done the trick. Yet the push here, the push there, the push in the right direction seldom came.

The Mark IV's and Mark V's moved quickly on from Schmidt to Kommerscheidt. Here officers and men of Major Hazlett's battalion of the 112th Infantry were trying frantically to halt the terrified men fleeing from Schmidt. In some cases, it took the persuasion of physical force and even pistol point to make the men join the Kommerscheidt defenders. "There was no holding them," said Staff Sgt. Frank Ripperdam of Company L. "They were pretty frantic and panicky." It took an hour and a half to corral as many as 200 men to augment the Kommerscheidt defenses.

Under these circumstances, another rout like that at Schmidt might have developed, but the troops in Kommerscheidt had something those at Schmidt had not had. They had, in the first place, artillery support on full alert. They had

also three Sherman tanks under an audacious young lieutenant named Fleig.

Maneuvering fearlessly from flank to flank, Ray Fleig and
his tanks knocked out three of the German tanks. A bomb from
a P-47 accounted for another, a rocket from a bazooka manned
by a company commander for a fifth. In mid-afternoon, the
Germans fell back from Kommerscheidt to rally under cover
of the buildings on the higher ground in Schmidt. To this
point, at least, Carl Peterson's prescience in providing a back-
up position in Kommerscheidt was paying off.

As the Germans fell back, the 28th Division commander,
General Cota, ordered Peterson to retake Schmidt. To someone in a rear command post looking at a map, it was a legitimate order. To someone on the ground—as Peterson and the
assistant division commander, Brig. Gen. George A. Davis,
discovered upon arriving at Kommerscheidt in late afternoon
—it was founded on illusion.

It was a strange order coming from "Dutch" Cota, a man
who ordinarily was not one to run his division from a command post. Cota had a reputation for satisfying himself first
by a look at the situation on the ground. What was the matter
now? Did the Huertgen Forest foster some psychological ma-
laise affecting soldier and commander alike?

Whatever the reason, this failure of Cota and his staff to
ascertain the true situation was the start of a condition that was
to have drastic consequences for the 28th Division through the
rest of the Huertgen Forest fight. Division headquarters lost
control of the battle, mainly through lack of information as to
what was going on at the foxhole level or through faulty and
misleading information, much of it designed to conceal the
extent of reverses. On the night of November 4, for example,
word reached Courtney Hodges at First Army headquarters
that the troops beyond the Kall had attacked during the
afternoon to retake Schmidt and had gained 300 yards. The
fact was that nobody had attacked and nobody had gained
anything. Indeed, so depleted was the force beyond the Kall
that there was no longer any question of attacking but of
trying to hold on to Kommerscheidt.

Untroubled by attacks elsewhere on the *Seventh Army* front, the hyperactive German army commander, Erich Brandenberger, took personal charge of the campaign to push back the 28th Division. Hans Schmidt's *275th Division*, Brandenberger directed, was to hold the wings of the American salient to prevent its widening. The *116th Panzer Division*'s panzer regiment, along with the *89th Division*, was to throw back all Americans from the east bank of the Kall. As for the rest of the panzer division, one regiment was to continue to try to dislodge the 109th Infantry from the woods near Huertgen while the other was building up in the woods opposite the Vossenack Ridge. After the engineers had improved a trail through the woods to provide passage for assault guns, this regiment was to retake Vossenack. Meanwhile, the panzer division's *Reconnaissance Battalion* was to drive down the Kall gorge to cut the American supply route across the Kall.

Despite the necessity for the Americans to get tanks and tank destroyers to Kommerscheidt, just over a company of engineers (out of an entire engineer group that was available if necessary) worked on the Kall trail during November 4, the day disaster struck at Schmidt. For fear of damaging some of the five disabled tanks blocking the trail, the engineers hesitated to use explosives on the troublesome rock outcroppings. Indeed, the tanks were treated with the kind of warm-hearted affection an old-time cavalryman might have lavished on a lame horse. Instead of pitching the tanks off the trail into the abyss, everybody worked, through the day of November 4 and far past midnight, at getting them moving again, but without the slightest success.

All day one report after another reached 28th Division headquarters asserting that the trail was open. Neither General Cota, Colonel Peterson, nor the 1171st Engineer Combat Group commander, Col. Edmund K. Daley, checked personally or sent a liaison officer to the spot until mid-afternoon, when Cota, disturbed by conflict between reports of inadequate support beyond the Kall and engineer assurances that the trail was open, ordered Daley to send what Cota called "a competent officer" to verify the condition of the trail. Daley in turn ordered the commander of the 20th Engineer Battalion to go personally into the gorge and take charge.

Two hours after midnight, Cota finally got fed up with the tankers' commendable but illogical struggle to save their tanks. Either clear the trail by daybreak, Cota ordered, or roll the tanks over the cliff. As the engineers set detonator caps to explosives against the troublesome rock outcroppings, Captain Hostrup and his crewmen nudged their vehicles into the abyss.

Soon after daylight on November 5, nine self-propelled tank destroyers and Hostrup's six remaining tanks crossed the Kall gorge. The men of the 112th Infantry, huddled miserably in rain-filled foxholes at Kommerscheidt, welcomed them like besieged settlers rescued from Indians by the U.S. cavalry. Unfortunately, their coming would prove to be less rescue than reprieve.

Presence of the tanks and destroyers at Kommerscheidt, plus the first genuinely clear day since the attack had begun, discouraged the German tanks from making another direct assault on Kommerscheidt. Every time a tank emerged from Schmidt, an American plane pounced on it. The panzer crewmen had to content themselves with firing from the shadows of buildings in Schmidt. Devastating though this fire was on the exposed foxholes around Kommerscheidt, it was insufficient to enable German infantry to drive the attack home.

On the same day, the Germans set out to reduce a second American force, numbering perhaps as many as 200 men. In fleeing Schmidt, these men had moved not to Kommerscheidt but into the woods southwest of Schmidt. Here officers among the group had organized a perimeter defense, but persistent German attacks gradually whittled down their numbers. Three days later, on November 7, three men would escape through the woods, eventually to make their way into American lines with the first news of the trapped group; but they were too late. On November 8 the Germans captured the survivors of the isolated force, 133 men.

Meanwhile, on November 5, other crises were building up. Against the 109th Infantry near Huertgen, German pressure continued all day, but the lines held. The 110th Infantry meanwhile engaged in persistent small-unit attacks to close the pillbox-studded gap between Raffelsbrand and Simonskall, but with no more success than before. Not for some days would anybody acknowledge the fact officially, but the forest already had sapped all offensive ability from this regiment.

It was at Vossenack and along the Kall trail that the more serious crises began to develop. On the exposed northeastern nose of the Vossenack Ridge, German shells threw ugly black plumes of dirt and the yellow smell of burning powder into the air. So shaky did the infantrymen become in their exposed foxholes that the assistant division commander, General Davis, ordered at least a platoon of tanks to stay in Vossenack at all times to bolster infantry morale.

Along the Kall trail, the crisis developed when the Germans began to accept the standing invitation to sever the supply route to Kommerscheidt.

Despite the provision that the 20th Engineers were to secure the Kall trail, the engineers had done nothing to comply until late on November 4, when they put a four-man guard at the bridge over the river and a company at the point southeast of Vossenack where the trail enters the woods. But these dispositions did almost nothing toward denying the bulk of the trail, as two squads of engineers who were working there found out during the night of November 5.

As the engineers worked, a German soldier suddenly appeared on the trail only fifteen feet away. Blowing shrilly on a whistle, he set off a rain of fire from machine guns and burp guns. Taken by surprise, the engineers had no chance. Those who survived did so only by melting into the woods.

A half-hour later, several Germans knocked at the door of a log-walled dugout alongside the trail that served as a medical aid station for the two battalions of the 112th Infantry beyond the Kall. Satisfying themselves that the medics were unarmed, the Germans posted a guard and left.

Two hours before daylight, as two jeeps left Vossenack with ammunition for Kommerscheidt, a German force loomed out of the darkness and opened fire with machine guns and a *Panzerfaust.*

"Shoot, man, shoot!" yelled a lieutenant to the soldier riding with him.

"I can't, Lieutenant," the man cried back; "I'm dying right here!"

As these events indicated, the enemy had moved uncontested into the Kall River gorge. Contradictory reports about the status of the Kall trail nevertheless continued to reach headquarters in the rear, so that it was not until well after daylight on November 6 that the engineer group commander, Colonel Daley, learned that the Germans had cut the trail. Daley promptly ordered the 20th Engineers to sweep the Germans from the woods. "Get every man you have into the line fighting," Daley thundered.

But as luck would have it, somebody else already had unwittingly set out to clear the Germans from the gorge.

Late the previous afternoon (November 5), General Cota had ordered the commander of the 707th Tank Battalion, Lt. Col. Richard W. Ripple, to form a special task force to help the 112th Infantry retake Schmidt. On paper, Ripple's strength looked impressive. He was to have a battalion of the 110th Infantry, one of his own medium tank companies, his light tank company, and a company of tank destroyers. Yet, in reality, Task Force Ripple was feeble. The stupefying fighting in the woods south of Richelskaul already had reduced the infantry battalion to little more than 300 weary men. The medium tank company was Captain Hostrup's, already beyond the Kall with but nine tanks left. The tank destroyers also were those already in Kommerscheidt, reduced now to seven guns.

Colonel Ripple and his 300 infantrymen reached the point where the Kall trail enters the woods southeast of Vossenack before daylight on the sixth, only minutes after the Germans had knocked out the two jeeps. Learning from the engineers that the Germans controlled the trail, Ripple decided to make his way to the river along a firebreak that paralleled the trail.

Even this proved difficult. Hardly had Ripple and the depleted infantry battalion entered the woods when they ran into men of the *116th Panzer Division's Reconnaissance Battalion*. But with a determination that had been all too rare in the 28th Division's fight, Ripple stuck to his assignment. Ordering the infantry to attack, he and his men fought their way foot by foot down the steep wooded slope to the Kall, then marched unimpeded up the opposite side of the gorge.

Nobody on the American side knew it at the time, but Task Force Ripple had, in effect, successfully counterattacked the panzer division's *Reconnaissance Battalion* and driven the Germans from the gorge. Not until later in the day would the Americans find it out, but the Kall trail again was open.

Task Force Ripple had not sufficient strength to make a similar impression on the Germans at Schmidt. So discouraged with the condition of the task force was the 112th Infantry commander, Colonel Peterson, that he saw little hope of retaking Schmidt.

Hardly had he issued the attack order and his subordinates begun their preattack reconnaissance when German fire cut down the commander of the newly arrived infantry battalion and three other key officers. Thoroughly discouraged, Peterson canceled the attack. He sent the battalion to dig in at the woods line behind Kommerscheidt to afford some strength in depth.

This was as close as the 28th Division would come to mounting an attack to retake Schmidt. Not that General Cota would not make another try. The next day, November 7, he created another task force under his assistant division commander, George Davis, but in much the same way as Task Force Ripple, this force was strong only on paper. When a depleted battalion of the 109th Infanty set out to secure a crossing of the Kall for Davis and his task force and ended up lost in the woods three miles away, it became more and more apparent to all concerned that nobody was going to retake Schmidt.

The 28th Division had enough trouble just trying to survive.

The harassed company commanders in Colonel Hatzfeld's 2d Battalion, 112th Infantry, on the naked northeastern nose of the Vossenack Ridge had been afraid something might happen.

Already they had reported to Hatzfeld that the continual German shelling had shattered their men's nerves, that some men had to be ordered to eat, that many of them cried like children. But nobody had done anything about it. The battalion commander himself sat in his command post in a basement in Vossenack, his head in his hands.

All was quiet on the ridge that morning of November 6. Strangely quiet, for every day heretofore the Germans at dawn had shelled the ridge heavily. In muddy, littered holes in the ground, men looked at each other nervously, and wondered.

A burp gun fired suddenly off to the left.

Somebody screamed, a piercing, agonizing, inexplicable scream.

Then it was quiet again.

A half-hour later, the German guns spoke, punishing the ridge with big, ugly, noisy explosions.

The men suddenly could stand no more. Panic-ridden, men of one company grabbed wildly at their equipment and broke for the rear. Seeing this company flee, the commander of the other forward company passed the word to his men to fall back on the battalion reserve at the edge of Vossenack. But it did not work. The impulse to run was a disease, a virulent, highly contagious disease that spread like the plague. Once started, the men would not stop. The reserve company too was caught up in the flight.

"[It was] the saddest sight I have ever seen," reported 1st Lt. James A. Condon of Company E. "Down the road from the east came men from F, G, and E Companies, pushing, shoving, throwing away equipment, trying to outrace the artillery and each other, all in a frantic effort to escape. They were all scared and excited. Some were terror-stricken. Some were helping the slightly wounded to run, and many of the badly wounded men, probably hit by the artillery, were lying in the road where they fell, screaming for help. It was a heartbreaking, demoralizing scene."

Nobody saw any Germans, but obviously the Germans were fast on their heels. Nobody knew where he was going either, only to some nebulous place of safety called "the rear."

The wild-eyed stampede had lost little momentum as it reached the battalion command post near the center of the village.

"They ran as fast as they could," recalled Capt. James T. Nesbitt, the battalion personnel officer. "Those we saw were completely shattered. . . . There was no sense fooling ourselves about it; it was a disorderly retreat. The men were going back pell-mell."

Dashing from the basement command post, officers of the battalion staff tried frantically to stem the retreat. They had little success. Trying to form a new line running through the center of the village near a shell-battered church, they could muster no more than seventy men. Even some of these melted away once the officers turned their backs.

Meanwhile, crewmen of a platoon of tank destroyers and a platoon of tanks in the northeastern edge of Vossenack watched in dismay as the infantrymen fled. Seeing no Germans, they held their ground. At last, in mid-morning, they fell back to the thin line established near the church.

As a matter of fact, there were no Germans. One of the *116th Panzer Division's* panzer grenadier regiments had been planning an attack to begin three hours before dawn, but the division engineers failed to improve the trail leading through the woods sufficiently to enable assault guns to participate. Even after the division commander, General von Waldenburg, ordered the attack to proceed without assault guns, a breakdown in communications between infantry and artillery forced another delay. Not until noon, several hours after the Americans had pulled out, did the Germans occupy the northeastern half of Vossenack.

War is not a pretty thing, even in victory. It is uglier still in defeat. It is at its ugliest when it invokes its awful power to cast brave men in the role of cowards. Twice now this had happened in the 28th Division's battle for Schmidt. This time it was not even an enemy attack that set it off; threat of attack alone had been enough. Here it was, at its ugliest and its most inexplicable, that mysterious mass contagion which through centuries of warfare has oftentimes gripped even the most experienced troops. It was ugly, incredible, but nonetheless real. The assistant division commander, General Davis, was in Germeter when the storm broke in Vossenack. Finding himself torn between two crises—that at Vossenack and that in the Kall gorge—he had only one place to turn for a reserve to influence either situation, to Colonel Daley's 1171st Engineer Combat Group.

Into Vossenack, to reinforce the thin line near the church, Davis sent the 146th Engineers, still wearing rubber hip boots they had been using against the mud in the forest. To the Kall gorge he sent the remnants of the 20th Engineers and two companies of the 1340th Engineers.

Meanwhile, commanders at higher echelons became markedly concerned about the crisis at Vossenack. Already, on November 5, the day after the 112th Infantry lost Schmidt, Courtney Hodges, along with Gerow of the V Corps and Collins of the VII Corps, had visited the 28th Division's command post, but there General Cota's optimistic plans to retake Schmidt with Task Force Ripple had allayed their concern. The threat at Vossenack was something else. Should the Germans break through into Germeter, they might split the 28th Division and even push through the forest to disrupt the First Army's main drive.

Hearing the news from Vossenack, Leonard Gerow promptly called on the 4th Division, which was en route to the VII Corps to participate in the main drive, to send a regiment to help. During the night, this regiment was to relieve the 109th Infantry at the woods line southwest of Huertgen, freeing the 109th for use at Vossenack and, Gerow hoped, for retaking Schmidt. It was this relief during the night of the sixth that led to the last, futile flurry of hope that the 28th Division might still regain Schmidt, a hope that would die the next day.

In Vossenack, as daylight came on November 7, the 146th Engineers and the panzer grenadier regiment of the *116th Panzer Division* were getting ready to push each other out of the village. It was the engineers who got started first. For all their unfamiliarity with the role of attacking infantry, the engineers moved with enthusiasm and energy. Close behind their artillery preparation, they dashed across a street near the church and began a systematic house-by-house advance. Whenever particularly stubborn resistance developed, a tank platoon advancing along the fringe of the village went into action. By nightfall this band of determined men held all of Vossenack. About them lay 150 dead and wounded of the panzer grenadier regiment.

The situation in the Kall gorge, meanwhile, was neither so quickly nor so decisively set right. As the men of the 1340th Engineers advanced down the Kall trail, they discovered with relief that the Germans had left, driven away earlier by Task Force Ripple; but even as the engineers dug in, the *116th Panzer Division's Reconnaissance Battalion* was getting set for a second move into the gorge.

Once again the engineers put a company into the relatively useless position where the Kall trail enters the woods, but this time they also put a company at the Kall bridge. This second company could have provided a genuine obstacle to enemy movement through the gorge. Yet when the Germans attacked just before midnight, most of the engineers faded away into the woods. Only the company commander and five men remained. Again the Germans were free to roam the gorge at will.

Fortunately for the Americans, this German unit appeared to be no more pertinacious than were the engineers. Even after the Germans cut the trail around midnight, an American supply column carrying rations and ammunition crossed and recrossed the Kall gorge. As daylight came on November 7, the situation along the trail was something of a paradox, the Germans claiming control of the gorge, yet American vehicles still able to cross the Kall.

Word that the engineers had deserted the position at the bridge did not reach the commander of the 1340th Engineers until after midday. He immediately ordered his third company to move to the bridge and "stay there." Passing down the firebreak paralleling the trail, this company left a platoon at the foot of the firebreak and established its main position astride the Kall trail west of the bridge. That part of the trail beyond the river still was unprotected, and even west of the river

German patrols would continue to look in on the aid station near the trail; but at long last an American unit was in position to provide at least a measure of protection for the trail.

Just how long the Americans would continue to have use for the trail was another question, for during the day of the seventh, events at Kommerscheidt had been fast striding to a climax. The issue beyond the Kall would not long be in doubt.

A reluctant dawn on November 7 brought with it a cold winter rain that turned foxholes into muddy ponds and further lowered the spirits of the weary men who for three days had held at Kommerscheidt. Then came a rain of German shells. For a full hour the shells came, one after another, in an incessant drumbeat of explosion. They left the gutted buildings of Kommerscheidt in flames, the infantrymen in a stupor.

From Schmidt rolled fifteen tanks and more than a battalion of infantry. Though the American tank destroyers knocked out five of the tanks, they paid with three destroyers and two of their own tanks. Still the Germans came on. By noon German tanks were cruising among the forward foxholes, shooting right and left with their big cannon and burying men under three feet of mud with their twisting, grinding steel hooves. The Americans began to give, not in a panic as at Schmidt and Vossenack, but to give nonetheless. Individually and in small groups, the men who could escape German fire began to race across open ground to the north to seek refuge in the reserve position at the woods line.

As a German tank stuck its cannon in the door of a house that was serving as command post for both American battalions in Kommerscheidt, the last resistance began to collapse. Sergeant Ripperdam of Company L saw it this way:

There was a hellish amount of noise and confusion and everyone was pretty nervous. I was feeling pretty low. Then the first thing I knew one of the boys said there was a big tank right on top of the battalion CP. We took off to have a look. I saw the tank on the CP, in a position to cover the entrance. . . . There were Americon soldiers in front of it and they had their hands raised in surrender. There was a white flag showing. . . . With this scene in our minds, we saw A and B Company men streaming back to the rear, running, but most of them still had their weapons. We took off and joined them.

As the first men arrived at the woods line, a message came over the 112th Infantry radio for the regimental commander, Colonel Peterson. Peterson, the radio operator said, was to report immediately to the division command post.

Peterson did not question the message. For a day now he had heard a rumor that he was to be relieved of his command, to be replaced by a colonel recently assigned to the division. What was more, Peterson was bitter. With his own eyes he had seen the men of his regiment—many of whom he had known almost since childhood—ripped to pieces on an assignment that Peterson believed had long ago become impractical without prompt and sizable reinforcements. Convinced that the true situation beyond the Kall never had reached the ears of General Cota, Peterson welcomed a chance to set the record straight.

Turning over his command to the next senior officer, the task force commander, Colonel Ripple, who himself was witness to receipt of the message, Peterson made his way down the steep wooded slope toward the Kall River. Wounded twice by German shellfire, he was semicoherent when engineers west of the Kall came upon him in late afternoon.

When medics carried him to an aid station near the division command post, Peterson, still dazed, demanded a word with the division commander, General Cota. Cota was appalled to see him. Though a new commander was, in fact, to join the 112th Infantry, he was not due to arrive for several days, and Cota himself had sent no message for Peterson to return. Tired from long days and sleepless nights, mentally exhausted from what was happening to his division, Cota could think only that Peterson had abandoned his troops under fire.

It was too much for Cota. He fainted.

Back at Kommerscheidt, in the meantime, Colonel Ripple found the situation in the village irretrievable. Left with but two tank destroyers and three tanks—one of them still commanded by the intrepid Lieutenant Fleig—the armored vehicles began to fall back. Any infantry that still remained took this as a cue to pull out.

The 28th Division's holdings beyond the Kall were reduced now to a small defensive perimeter at the woods line northwest of Kommerscheidt where the Kall trail emerges from the woods. This nobody actually on the scene had any hope of holding for long, and, for once, those away from the scene saw it the same way.

Talking with General Gerow by telephone, Cota asked the V Corps commander for permission to fall back behind the Kall. Gerow in turn called Hodges at First Army headquarters. In an unusual step, General Hodges insisted first on getting the opinion of the assistant division commander, General Davis, a reflection of Hodges' confidence in Davis, who once had served on his staff, but an affront nevertheless to Cota. In the end, Hodges gave his approval.

So long as the commanders at both corps and army believed it less important to reinforce the 28th Division for retaking Schmidt than to hold on to their strength for the projected big offensive, no one could argue that anything was to be gained by trying to maintain a foothold beyond the Kall. Had anybody recognized the true importance of Schmidt and the Roer River Dams, they might well have chosen to spare some other force for retaking Schmidt. At least, they might have committed the combat command of armor that throughout the 28th Division's troubles had stood ready but uncalled upon in the Monschau Corridor. But this was not how it was in early November 1944.

The next day, November 8, while a new commander for what remained of the 112th Infantry made his way beyond the Kall with orders to pull everybody back during the night, the fate that had befallen the 28th Division brought a galaxy of American commanders to Cota's command post. Not only Gerow and Hodges but the army group commander, General Bradley, and the Supreme Commander, General Eisenhower, attended. But their conference at this point was more a postmortem than a timely consultation on how to get the patient on his feet.

The second attack on Schmidt had developed into one of the most costly actions to be fought by a United States division during World War II. The 112th Infantry alone lost 167 men killed, 431 missing (most of whom were later declared killed), 232 captured, 719 wounded, and 544 hospitalized for "nonbattle" causes, including combat exhaustion and respiratory diseases.

The entire 28th Division, including attached units, incurred 6,184 casualties. The Germans lost about half that number.

Though parts of the 28th Division continued to attack for another five days in an effort to seize the rest of the woods line overlooking Huertgen and to conquer the pillboxes at Raffelsbrand, these were prodigious assignments far beyond the means of a unit which had taken such a physical and spiritual beating as had the 28th Division. When the division at last was relieved and moved to a relatively quiet defensive sector in the Ardennes (there to be hit a month later by the winter counteroffensive), the lines remained basically what they had been after the third day's fighting, except that nobody now stood beyond the Kall.

The tragic outcome of the 28th Division's attack meant that Courtney Hodges had to settle for a flank anchored not on the upper Roer but on the Kall. It also meant that the commanding ground at Schmidt and the tactical ace of the Roer River Dams remained in German hands. Though the nature of the German reaction to the 28th Division's attack made clear for the first time to top American commanders something of the true value of the dams, the First Army still failed to do anything specific about capturing or destroying them.

TO BREAK THE IMPASSE

12   THAT A MAJOR American offensive was soon to be launched in the Aachen sector could come as no surprise to the Germans. The very logic of it would see to that, even had the Germans chosen to ignore the arrival of a new army—Simpson's Ninth—north of Aachen; to obvious concentration of the First Army; and to the 28th Division's preliminary thrust to take Schmidt and—the Germans had come to believe—the Roer River Dams.

Nor were the Germans necessarily to be pitied for what they now could muster to oppose the new offensive. Only in November was German war production reaching a peak, and one new *volksgrenadier* division after another was being outfitted for either the Eastern or Western Front. Even as the Germans built up their defensive strength, they had enough left over to create the steel heart of the reserve force that in December was destined to strike in the Ardennes.

While this reserve consisting primarily of panzer divisions was being formed, Hitler allowed a kind of round-robin temporary use of the new *volksgrenadier* divisions, to insure that the Americans did not advance beyond the Roer River. He also permitted use of new artillery corps and *Nebelwerfer* brigades. Granted a fairly liberal ration of artillery ammunition, these units enabled the Germans to build up a potent artillery arm.

Because the winter counteroffensive was to be concealed from friend and foe alike, the Germans adopted an elaborate system of justifying every build-up for the counteroffensive in terms of "the anticipated enemy offensive." Thus, when Hitler early in November transferred the *Sixth Panzer Army* from the East to take charge of the panzer reserve for the counteroffensive, every order connected with the move pointed to it as a stratagem aimed at countering the big American offensive from Aachen. Hardly anyone on either the American or even the German side below the level of army commander knew otherwise.

In another move that furthered the deception, Field Marshal von Rundstedt, the Commander in Chief in the West, in late October shifted to the Aachen sector the headquarters of the *Fifth Panzer Army*. Commanded by one of Hitler's ablest tank experts, General der Panzertruppen Hasso von Manteuffel, this headquarters assumed temporary responsibility for the north wing of Brandenberger's *Seventh Army*. This involved taking over the sector of the *81st Corps* in the Stolberg Corridor and another corps farther north, leaving Brandenberger with the job of defending only the Eifel from Schevenhuette south. It had the virtue not only of reducing Brandenberger's overextended front but of putting an expert on armored warfare in charge of preparing the defenses to oppose the American main effort.

Deception entered the picture when on the eve of the American offensive Manteuffel and his *Fifth Panzer Army* headquarters disengaged secretly, retiring behind the Roer River to get ready for the counteroffensive. Meanwhile, headquarters of the *Fifteenth Army* moved in similar secrecy from Holland, leaving behind both its sector and its name to a new headquarters and taking over not only Manteuffel's sector but the name *Gruppe von Manteuffel* as an alias.

Thus the American main effort was to strike a sector commanded by General der Infanterie Gustav von Zangen—a strong-willed, handsome Teutonic type, two-time winner of the Knight's Cross, who long had headed the *Fifteenth Army*

—but a sector which most Germans themselves believed to be commanded by General von Manteuffel. The bulk of the Huertgen Forest remained the responsibility of Brandenberger and his *Seventh Army*, but Zangen and *Gruppe von Manteuffel* were charged with the northern tip of the forest around Schevenhuette and the purlieus of the forest in the Stolberg Corridor.

In this realignment, the Germans in the Aachen sector gained a reserve, a panzer corps with one panzer division and one panzer grenadier division. This reserve Field Marshal Model at *Army Group B* located not opposite the Stolberg Corridor, where the Americans actually planned their main effort, but farther north in the more open ground of the Roer Plain, opposite the Ninth U.S. Army. For to the Germans it was incredible that the Americans would make their main thrust in the broken, semiforested terrain of the Stolberg Corridor and the adjacent Huertgen Forest. They anticipated the main effort on the Roer Plain and would continue to believe the main effort located there, even after the offensive began.

On the American side, the 12th Army Group commander, General Bradley, had chosen the First Army rather than the Ninth for his main effort for two basic reasons. The First Army was an established, experienced force, while the Ninth Army was untried. Furthermore, because the British to the north were not to attack until some time after Bradley's offensive began, the Ninth Army would be Bradley's exterior force. In Bradley's book of rules, one did not entrust one's main effort to an exterior force.

Having drawn the assignment of "main effort," Joe Collins' VII Corps was reinforced strongly with artillery and also was to receive the benefit of a preponderance of a preattack air bombardment of unparalleled proportions. Called Operation QUEEN, the air attack was to be a "carpet bombing" patterned after the bombardment that had preceded the breakout from Normandy. Not only fighter-bombers and medium bombers but the big strategic bombers—American and British—were to participate in a tactical air attack on an unprecedented scale.

Directly in front of the VII Corps, three heavy-bomber divisions (more than 1,200 planes) of the Eighth U.S. Air Force were to lay waste the city of Eschweiler and its environs just outside the northern reaches of the Stolberg Corridor and the industrial town of Langerwehe at the tip of the Huertgen Forest. An equal number of Royal Air Force heavies were to punish Dueren and two other communications centers on the Roer farther downstream. Approximately 600 medium bombers of the Ninth U.S. Air Force were to attack troops, field installations, and smaller communications centers in the Stolberg Corridor and in front of the Ninth Army. In general, fighter-bombers were to operate on call from front-line divisions. Counting American and British fighters flying escort protection for the big bombers, Operation QUEEN was to employ more than 4,500 planes, approximately half of them heavy bombers.

An aerial attack of this magnitude in direct support of troops on the ground required elaborate systems of electronic and visual control. Though these systems were worked out in immense detail to insure that bombs would not fall short on American positions, both ground and air commanders remained concerned lest all precautions fail and the tragic errors that had been made in Normandy should be made again. So concerned were the commanders that they grew overcautious. They designated a bomb line two miles beyond American positions, more than three times the safety margin allowed in Normandy, so that many questioned whether the ground troops could traverse the two miles quickly enough to capitalize on the shock effect of the bombardment.

In the VII Corps, Joe Collins was to have two fresh divisions for his attack. These were the relatively new 104th Division, which took over the line around Stolberg and was to attack northeast, outside the Stolberg Corridor, and the veteran 4th Division. The latter moved deep into the Huertgen Forest, taking over the line of engineer roadblocks between Schevenhuette and the 28th Division's positions near Huertgen. Reinforced by CCR of the 5th Armored Division, the 4th Division was to push northeast directly through the forest to reach the Roer River at Dueren.

The main effort of the VII Corps General Collins entrusted to the 1st Division and an attached regiment, the 9th Division's 47th Infantry. The 1st Division, known from its shoulder patch as the "Big Red One," the most experienced of all units in the corps, had had time to rest since conquering Aachen. The division was to attack from Schevenhuette through the tip of the Huertgen Forest and through the northeastern reaches of the Stolberg Corridor to gain the open country of the Roer Plain and sweep to the Roer north of Dueren. Collins' remaining division, the 3d Armored under Maurice Rose, was to be held in reserve.

To many a commander and common soldier alike, the projected attack by the VII Corps and the companion piece by the Ninth Army had all the trappings of a breakthrough operation on a grand scale. Three of the top commanders involved, Collins, Hodges, and Bradley, were openly optimistic. For the ebullient Collins, this was normal, but the usually conservative Hodges and Bradley were equally cheerful. Not even the miserable November weather nor the disaster that befell the 28th Division as the main forces waited could dim the optimism.

Though it would take the opening of Antwerp late in the month to remove all logistical problems, extraordinary efforts by supply and transport units had produced such spectacular results that by the end of the first week of November few supply shortages existed. Replacements had brought all units up to strength. Behind the lines, artillery pieces stood in some places almost hub to hub, trucks churned to and fro, and word passed from man to man that the planes were coming—the big ones.

What was more, the men on the whole were rested, equipment and weapons cleaned and oiled, tanks and tank destroyers replaced or repaired. Not since Aachen capitulated to the 1st Division on October 21 had any unit now in the VII Corps made an attack, and most units had held relatively inactive positions since the September drive had bogged down.

Foxholes were covered from the rain, either with logs topped by tent tarpaulins or with doors or lumber taken from

German dwellings. A man had a chance to read the troop newspaper, *The Stars & Stripes*, to ogle the pin-up girls in the troop magazine, *Yank*, or to peruse any number of dehydrated overseas versions of home-front magazines. Quartermaster bakeries increased the issue of fresh white bread, and company kitchens three times a day sent forward palatable food kept hot in insulated cans.

Whenever possible, all divisions rotated battalions in the line, giving most men a night or two in a dry place a few hundred yards behind the front. Almost every regiment set up showers, run on the order of an assembly line, where a dirty man entered one end of a tent or converted building and emerged at the other end clean. Division, corps, and army rest centers sprang up in cities beyond normal range of artillery fire, eventually to provide almost every front-line soldier a resting place for forty-eight hours where liquor and female companionship were almost always in short supply but where blue-uniformed Red Cross girls dispensed doughnuts and coffee and where touring USO shows gave vaudeville a new lease on life. A few lucky men even got brief passes to Paris. There, the returning boulevardiers assured anybody who would listen, liquor and girls were no problem.

Everything now depended on the weather. The original target date of November 10 passed with rain. The next day, leaden skies. Already rain far in excess of normal had fallen. Streams were approaching flood level. Roads were rapidly deteriorating. The faltering 28th Division, having played a dreadful prologue to the main drama, had begun to stumble off the stage. Still no break in the weather. The thirteenth passed. Then the fourteenth. No break on the fifteenth either.

As night came on November 15, the forecast for the next day was again discouraging. Commanders and troops alike could only pray for a miracle, for by the terms of General Bradley's directive the offensive was to start the next day even if the weather had not cleared enough to permit the big air attack.

D day was November 16, regardless.

BREAKTHROUGH OR
SLUGGING MATCH?

13 BEYOND Schevenhuette, the wooded highlands of the Huertgen Forest reluctantly give way to the Roer Plain. The little Wehe Creek, which begins as the Weisser Weh in Deadman's Moor, cuts a deep swath to the northeast to delineate the forest proper from its purlieus. Dense patches of woods dot the land beyond the creek, and the ground is high and marked by rounded hillocks providing sharp observation advantages to the outskirts of the industrial town of Langerwehe and the abrupt start of the plain. The two most marked features of the high ground are Hill 203, overlooking Langerwehe, and a generally treeless ridge rising near the village of Hamich, a mile north of Schevenhuette.

It was this ridge and particularly its highest point—Hill 232, just outside the village of Hamich—which most occupied the 1st Division commander, Maj. Gen. C. Ralph Huebner, in making his plans for the big offensive. The 1st Division had to have Hill 232, if not the entire ridge, in order to move along the high ground left of the Wehe Creek and thereby help open a highway running from Schevenhuette close alongside the creek.

The enemy here still was Gerhard Engel's *12th Division.* In recognition for having stopped the VII U.S. Corps in September, Engel had been promoted to general and the division upgraded from infantry to *volksgrenadier* status. The division still constituted the south wing of the *81st Corps* and thus the south wing of General von Zangen's *Fifteenth Army* masquerading under the alias *Gruppe von Manteuffel*.

The *81st Corps* now had a new commander, General der Infanterie Friedrich J. M. Koechling, a man who handled his command assignments with the same imperturbability he had displayed in his peacetime profession as a circus acrobat. Koechling had replaced Friedrich-August Schack in late September after Brandenberger and Model, dissatisfied with Schack's handling of Schwerin's intransigence at Aachen, had granted Schack rest and recuperation leave. This was a polite way of saying *heraus* to a man without damaging his career.

The *81st Corps* had two other divisions in addition to the *12th*, both in the line farther north, opposite contingents of the Ninth U.S. Army. Besides a battalion or so held out in each division, the corps had no reserve.

As a part of the Hitler-approved round robin of reliefs to get ready for the winter counteroffensive, Engel's *12th Division* was earmarked for early replacement by a new unit, the *47th Volks Grenadier Division*. Commanded by Generalleutnant Max Bork, the *47th* had drawn roughly half its men from the *Luftwaffe* and the navy, and the other half from new levies of seventeen-year-olds and eighteen-year-olds, sprinkled with a few hoary veterans of the Russian front.

Shortly after midnight on November 15, General Hodges of the First U.S. Army gave the word to start the offensive that both Americans and Germans knew was coming. Though discouraged by weather forecasts that made it look as if the big air program would have to be canceled, Hodges had no choice. The sixteenth was the deadline date.

Yet even without large-scale air support, Hodges still could be optimistic, for he and General Simpson of the Ninth Army were to share in the first assault the equivalent of seven divisions. An armored division was immediately available within the VII Corps to back up the assault. The attack might be reinforced by three more corps, encompassing three armored and eight infantry divisions. Whether the skies cleared or not, 1,246 artillery pieces in all were to participate in the preliminary bombardment. In support of Collins' VII Corps alone were more than 300 tanks and tank destroyers and thirty-two battalions of field artillery. A VII Corps intelligence section, somewhat chastened by the stubborn German defense through September and October, nevertheless could point to a ratio of attacker to defender of almost 5 to 1. Only the possibility that the Germans might call in the panzer reserve they presumably were assembling near Cologne gave anybody on the American side any real pause.

Dawn on November 16 brought a day that at first looked like another siege of ragged clouds, overcast, and mists that did nothing to brighten the drab, dull, gray landscape. Yet by midmorning it was obvious even to the least optimistic that the clouds were thinning. A firm wind from the northwest picked up speed. Unknown to the infantrymen, the wind already had cleared the skies above the bases of the big bombers back in England. A half-hour before noon, the first of the big planes appeared.

Though fog continued to cling to most of the medium-bomber and fighter-bomber bases on the Continent, Operation QUEEN was on. For all the limitations imposed by weather, it was destined to be the largest air attack in direct support of ground troops in all of World War II.

Almost 1,200 heavy bombers of the Eighth U.S. Air Force dropped more than 4,000 tons of bombs on Eschweiler, just outside the Stolberg Corridor, and on Langerwehe; while an almost equal number of Royal Air Force heavies dropped more than 5,500 tons on three Roer River cities, almost half the total on Dueren. On the other hand, only eighty medium bombers reached the scene, and sorties by fighter aircraft also were limited. In front of the VII Corps, pilots of the Ninth TAC nevertheless flew 212 sorties, mostly against the Hamich Ridge and the village of Huertgen. During the course of the day, over 4,000 planes unloaded a total of more than 10,000 tons of bombs.

Grand and terrible and awe-inspiring the air attack was, without a doubt. Impressive, too, were the safety precautions, for in only one case, when four bombs killed one man and wounded two in a 3d Armored Division artillery battery, did the bombs inflict casualties on American units. Just how effective the attack had been in helping the ground troops through the German defenses was another question.

Because the bomb line was so far in front of friendly troops, few of the enemy's forward positions took any punishment. Even those German troops in support positions incurred few casualties, for most either found cover deep in cellars or already had burrowed deep in the earth for protection. The effect on communications and supplies was another matter. Telephone lines went out everywhere, and for days afterward German units were without hot food because of loss of kitchens, supply vehicles, and horses. Dueren looked like a Roman ruin, hundreds of soldiers and civilians entombed beneath its rubble. Partly because of the safety precautions, partly because the bombardment was spread over several miles of front, and partly because of poor visibility, the results of the air attack clearly bore no comparison to those of the concentrated blow that had helped American troops to break out of Normandy.

The most dramatic and damaging single event of the air attack directly affected the front opposite the 1st Division. Here fate dealt a cruel blow to the *47th Volks Grenadier Division.* Even as Allied planes struck, contingents of this division were getting off trains in the Roer cities, and some battalions were actually in the process of relieving units of the *12th Division.* "I never saw anything like it," said a German sergeant. "These kids were still numb forty-five minutes after the bombardment. It was our luck that your ground troops did not attack us until the next day. I could not have done anything with those boys of mine that day." It was even worse for an artillery battalion that was getting off trains along the Roer. The battalion was all but annihilated.

Some planes were still dropping their loads when American artillery opened fire, an hour before the ground troops were to move. In some ways as awesome as the aerial bombardment, the artillery attack came as close as any in World War II to the mammoth preparations that were the rule in World

War I. In front of the VII Corps alone, 694 guns fired almost 52,000 rounds. In addition, hundreds of tank and tank-destroyer pieces, plus 81mm. and 4.2-inch chemical mortars, contributed to the preparation. The ill-starred *47th Volks Grenadier Division* came in for a special share of this pounding, for a prisoner taken earlier in the day had alerted American artillery to the German plan to relieve the *12th Division*. Artillery commanders shifted much of their fire to routes likely to be used by the incoming troops.

It was a tremendous display of air and artillery power, but the test was yet to come. What would it be like when the infantrymen rose from their holes?

Soon after 12:45 P.M., when the ground attack began, the infantrymen learned the answer.

The Germans were still there.

Men of the 1st Battalion, 16th Infantry, commanded by Lt. Col. Edmund F. Driscoll, had scarcely entered the woods north of Schevenhuette when they ran into determined fire from the kind of log-covered emplacements everybody had come to associate with the Huertgen Forest. Only after a platoon of tanks had inched through clinging mud to the woods line to take out the enemy's automatic weapons could the battalion advance.

Reaching the edge of the woods overlooking Hamich as dusk approached, Colonel Driscoll could see at first hand the importance of Hill 232. So long as the Germans held that hill, not even a field mouse could sneak into Hamich unseen. After one futile attempt to break into the first houses, Driscoll and his men holed up for the night along the woods line to await tank support before trying again.

It was mid-morning the next day, November 17, before the attached 47th Infantry at last cleared a roundabout road leading to Hamich and a platoon of tanks could come forward. In early afternoon, tanks and infantry attacked together, but again to no avail. The small-arms fire from Hamich itself was bad, but the major problem was artillery fire, obviously adjusted from Hill 232.

Not until the third day, November 18, after clearing weather enabled fighter aircraft to hit Hill 232 and after the 16th Infantry commander sent another infantry battalion to help, did anybody get into the first houses of Hamich. There remained a systematic house-to-house, cellar-to-cellar killing match that did not end until mid-afternoon. Thereupon, the regimental commander, Col. Frederick W. Gibb, sent his remaining battalion against Hill 232 on the heels of a TOT* fired by fifteen field artillery battalions. Defending infantrymen of the *12th Division* were too dazed from the shelling to put up any kind of a fight. Graves registration units later were to remove twelve truckloads of German dead from the hill.

Knowing the German penchant for counterattack, few in the 16th Infantry could have expected to get away with taking a critical terrain feature like Hill 232 without some effort by the Germans to regain it. The Germans would, in fact, begin assembling troops for the task soon after nightfall on the eighteenth, but their effort was destined to be seriously affected by the perennial problem of maintaining direction in the confusing Huertgen Forest.

On the German side, hardly had the big offensive begun when Gustav von Zangen, commander of the *Fifteenth Army* (alias *Gruppe von Manteuffel*) canceled relief of the *12th Division* by the *47th Volks Grenadiers*. General Bork was to assemble his *47th Division* as a corps reserve, to be reinforced by a small task force from the *116th Panzer Division*, brought up from the dying battle near Huertgen. Higher German commanders otherwise made no immediate moves affecting this part of the front, for the big worry as they saw it was farther north against the Ninth U.S. Army.

A change in this procedure coincided with loss of Hill 232. Anxious to gain greater concentration farther north, Field Marshal Model at *Army Group B* looked covetously on the *47th Division*, but he hesitated to commit this green unit, already severely battered by the Allied bombardment, against what he thought was the American main effort. He ordered instead that

---

* Time-on-Target, a method of timing artillery fire from various points to fall on a given target simultaneously.

Zangen use the *47th* to take over the southern half of the *12th Division's* sector, thereby enabling all divisions in the *81st Corps* to make corresponding shifts northward.

The strings removed from use of the *47th Division,* Zangen immediately ordered a counterattack to retake Hill 232. Two battalions, reinforced by the task force of the *116th Panzer Division,* were to assemble during the night in the woods near the hill, then strike two hours before dawn the next morning, November 19.

Since the tanks and halftracks of the *116th Panzer's* task force were to be divided equally between the two infantry battalions, the task force moved forward after nightfall in two columns. One column made it to the assembly area without incident, but a lieutenant guiding the other column lost his way in the darkness. Unwittingly, he took a road leading from the Wehe Creek valley toward Hamich, directly into positions held by troops of the 16th Infantry outside the village.

It was men of Company C in foxholes astride the road who first heard the Germans approach. Reduced to but forty-five men in the fighting for Hamich, the company nevertheless opened fire with a vengeance; but in the face of the German tanks, this little band obviously could not have held for long. Fortunately, the German lieutenant, horrified at his error, drew back the column.

Still trying to reach his assembly area, the lieutenant next tried a trail leading north into the woods, but the trail twisted and turned, eventually leading again to Hamich. As the column came a second time under American fire, the lieutenant tried once more to disengage, but this time the confusion was too great. He had no choice but to order the column to try to bull its way through Hamich in what was, in effect, an impromptu attack.

Within Hamich, men of the 16th Infantry adopted the stratagem of taking cover in buildings and cellars while blanketing the entire village with artillery fire. Though the German halftracks and accompanying infantry beat a hasty retreat, the tanks pushed on. In the confusion, two tanks blundered into bomb craters. Unable to extricate them from the craters, the crews fled. A bazooka rocket fired from a window accounted for another tank, while several other tanks raced all the way through the village to escape to the north.

As the noise and confusion abated, the sole prisoner taken during the engagement turned out to be the hapless lieutenant. Shaken by his experience, he poured out the story of his misfortune and in the process gave away the entire counterattack plan. American artillery took the enemy officer at his word and brought the German assembly area under heavy fire, dooming the counterattack before it had even started. Alerted infantrymen in Hamich and on Hill 232 quickly finished off the effort.

With Hill 232 secured, the 16th Infantry soon after daylight on November 19 was at last in a position to continue northeast to take the high ground alongside the Wehe Creek and help open the highway in the valley. Meanwhile, on an assignment equally vital for much the same reason, the 26th Infantry had been attacking northeast through the woods on the other side of the creek. This regiment's first objective was a series of four densely wooded hills surrounding a small castle, the Laufenburg, roughly half the distance from Schevenhuette to Langerwehe.

Like many another unit that fought full within the Huertgen Forest, the 26th Infantry engaged from the first in an almost unalloyed small-arms battle. Limited observation severely restricted the effectiveness of artillery support, and the mud and a dearth of roads denied help from tanks and tank destroyers. The inevitable hazards of forest fighting—shellbursts in the trees and open flanks—plagued the regiment from the start. As always, the Germans gave ground grudgingly from log bunkers and log-covered foxholes cleverly camouflaged among the trees. The only difference between the 26th Infantry's fight and that of other units deeper in the forest was the nature of the forest itself, here predominantly deciduous rather than coniferous. In daytime, some of the murky November light peeked through.

For three days, first one battalion of the 26th Infantry, then another, ploughed slowly forward, gaining only a few hundred yards each day, then working like anguished beavers to "button up," as the saying had it, for the night. Then, early on the fourth day, November 19, a battalion of Max Bork's *47th Volks Grenadier Division,* entering the fight as part of the general commitment of that division, launched a sharp counterattack. Its force seriously depleted by three days in the woods, the 26th Infantry was hard put to stave off this counterattack. Yet hardly had the Germans begun to fall back when the first big break in the forest fighting developed. Acting the moment the Germans gave indication of withdrawing, the regimental commander, Col. John F. R. Seitz, thrust his reserve battalion into the breach. A German defense that only a few hours before had been tough and unyielding now gave like some soft, pliable thing. With a rush, the American infantrymen pushed almost a mile ahead, and gained a dirt road that leads into the forest from the Wehe Creek. The men of the 26th Infantry now stood only a few hundred yards from the Laufenburg, the castle encircled by the high ground the regiment was after.

A slight additional effort might well have carried the men to the objective, but the regimental commander, John Seitz, was cautious. The four gruelling days in the forest had made Seitz uncomfortably conscious of the lack of any kind of a supply road other than muddy, tree-strewn firebreaks. Not even jeeps towing 57mm. antitank guns could inch a way to the forward foxholes, and now that the men had reached a road that German tanks or assault guns might use, this fact took on new meaning. That the regiment had already lost some 450 men in the forest heightened Colonel Seitz' concern. Not until he got physical possession of the road up the Wehe Creek valley, Seitz believed, would it be wise to move on the hills and the Laufenburg. The division commander, Ralph Huebner, agreed.

As night came on November 19, General Huebner could point to definite breaks in the situation in front of both his committed regiments, the 16th Infantry at Hamich and Hill 232, and the 26th Infantry in the forest. Huebner could take heart, too, from the fact that his reserve regiment was still fresh and the attached 47th Infantry relatively so.

On the other hand, it had taken four days and over a thousand casualties to get this far. Under ordinary circumstances, this might have been less than discouraging, but these were not ordinary circumstances. The 1st Division was making the main effort of a corps, which was in turn making the main effort of an army, which in turn was making the main effort of an army group.

If one looked at the situation from the level of the corps commander, General Collins, the conclusion was much the same. In the Stolberg Corridor between the 1st and 104th Divisions, a combat command of the 3d Armored Division had cleared four villages on open ground below the Hamich Ridge, but even with the weight of armor, it had taken three days to accomplish the task. Furthermore, the 104th Division had required three days to capture a hill near Stolberg, so that not until the fourth day, November 19, had this division begun to make substantial progress outside the Stolberg Corridor. Then, too, the 4th Division, in the dark recesses of the Huertgen Forest, had run into the usual problems of forest fighting. Nor was the news appreciably different from the divisions of the Ninth Army on the Roer Plain.

By November 19, the optimism that had preceded the mammoth aerial bombardment and the start of the big, long-awaited offensive to jump the Roer River and gain the Rhine had begun to fade. In Normandy, by way of contrast, at a comparable period four days after the start of the breakthrough attempt, the forward troops were more than ten miles beyond the starting line. On November 19, the First and Ninth Armies were, on the average, no more than two miles from the jump-off point.

The American command had bargained for a dramatic breakthrough. After four days of fighting, it looked very much as if they had bought, instead, a drab slugging match.

THE GLOOM AND THE MISERY:
THE 4TH DIVISION

14 THE 4TH DIVISION in the Huertgen Forest had one
strike against it even before the November offensive began.
The cold, wet night of November 6—the night after men
of the 112th Infantry had abandoned the nose of the Vossenack
Ridge—the 4th Division had been on the march to join the VII
Corps for the big offensive when Leonard Gerow looked about
for some force to augment the 28th Division. To release the
109th Infantry to help at Vossenack and retake. Schmidt, he
radioed the 4th Division commander, Maj. Gen. Raymond O.
Barton, to drop off a regiment from his column.

Alarmed at the recurring crises in the 28th Division, Gerow
moved too fast. There would be no time for officers of the incoming regiment to reconnoiter or perform any of the other
tasks the army field manuals label essential for successful relief
under fire. The regiment, Gerow directed, was to move into the
Huertgen Forest immediately, that same night—the cold, wet,
dark-as-pitch night of November 6.

From this moment the fate of the 12th Infantry, the regiment that drew the assignment, was sealed. The commander,
Col. James S. Luckett, had no choice but to relieve the 109th
Infantry in place, unit for unit, no opportunity to improve the
crazy-quilt dispositions that attack and counterattack had imposed. Once he had dispersed his battalions and companies in

this manner, the forest and the Germans would see to it that they never got together again to form a cohesive striking force. Cold, wet, scared, night-blind, stumbling, swearing, falling, sweating, the men somehow plodded forward, over the mutilated limbs of the tall firs, over the stiff bodies of those who had come before them, up the slippery slopes, across the muddy firebreaks, into strange, dirty holes in the ground, into the night.

Colonel Luckett and the 12th Infantry were to do two of the jobs the 109th Infantry had failed to execute. They were to seize the woods line east of the Germeter–Huertgen highway, thereby gaining the rest of the originally assigned line of departure overlooking Huertgen. They also were to eliminate the enemy's dangerous countersalient in the valley of the Weisser Weh.

The 12th Infantry accomplished neither.

For three days the men tried, but the severe limitations imposed by the hasty commitment and by the proximity of the enemy denied any semblance of co-ordinated attack. On the fourth day, November 10, even as Generals Gerow and Collins were returning the regiment to the control of its parent division, the 12th Infantry tried again. This time Luckett and his men ended up fighting for their lives.

Having eliminated the 28th Division's penetrations beyond the Kall River, Siegfried von Waldenburg and his *116th Panzer Division* were free to turn full attention to the second part of their counterattack mission. This was pushing through the woods near Huertgen to cut off the American penetration at its base after the manner of *Regiment Wegelein*. While tanks and assault guns provided fire support from Huertgen, the panzer grenadiers moved to the attack soon after daylight on the tenth.

Catching the American infantry by surprise in attack formation, the Germans quickly surrounded two companies. For a time it looked as if they might push all the way south to Germeter and perhaps beyond. Only by hastily contriving a new defensive line deep in the woods was the rest of the 12th Infantry able to hold on to as much as a third of the gains earlier achieved by the 109th. Two days later, on November 12, when two other companies at last broke through to the encircled companies, the Germans closed in behind them too.

It was during this action that one of the most diabolical incidents to occur in the battle of the Huertgen Forest took place. In the fighting late on the tenth, a soldier from Company B lay alone in the forest, seriously wounded. Three Germans found him, took his cigarettes, his watch, rifled his pockets, then rigged underneath him an explosive charge set to go off whenever anybody picked the man up.

For seventy hours this man lay alone in the cold, wet forest, suffering torture from his wound almost to the point of delirium but fighting with every ounce of strength he could muster to keep awake, to maintain consciousness lest someone come to his aid and inadvertently blow him and his rescuers to kingdom come. Incredibly, when rescuers found him, the man still had strength to call out a warning. The man lived, a testament to the courage and endurance of the human spirit.

Not until November 15, the very eve of the big offensive, was Colonel Luckett able to extricate his four encircled companies and bring them back to a defensive line deep in the woods, almost the same line the 109th Infantry had used for its jump-off far back on the second day of November. In nine days of incredibly bitter fighting, the 12th Infantry had lost ground rather than gained it. More than 1,600 men had fallen victim either to enemy fire, combat exhaustion, or an insidious enemy called "trench foot." The latter was a serious malady with symptoms akin to frostbite that reached epidemic proportions as men lived long days and nights in cold and wet, unable to clean or dry their feet. Feet swelled, toes turned purple, and sometimes amputation was the only recourse.

Though higher commanders stubbornly refused to accept the fact for some days to come, the 12th Infantry for the time being could contribute no more to the main offensive than had the 110th Infantry to taking the pillboxes at Raffelsbrand. Spent, beaten, all but demoralized, their eyes glassy, set in drawn white masks of faces, the men of the 12th Infantry nevertheless drew an assignment to attack on the big day, November 16. The regiment was to regain the ground it had lost and establish control over either the Germeter–Huertgen highway or the roadnet in the valley of the Weisser Weh. Once a road was opened, Combat Command R of the 5th Armored Division was to pass through to take the village of Huertgen.

To those on the scene who knew the true condition of the 12th Infantry, it could have come as no surprise that the regiment failed to come even close to attaining these objectives. Only in the valley of the Weisser Weh were the men able to gain any ground, and there only a few hundred yards. This dismal failure cost Colonel Luckett his command. To the credit of his superior, General Barton, Luckett nevertheless retained his rank and received command of a regiment in another division.

With the 12th Infantry taking a beating in the woods southwest of Huertgen, the 4th Division had only two regiments left—two regiments with which to attack on a four-mile front, penetrate three and a half miles of Huertgen jungle, then continue another three and a half miles to the Roer River. Even with the assignment of the 5th Armored's CCR to take the village of Huertgen, the task was staggering. General Barton—a man with a heavy moustache and a build that brought him the nickname "Tubby," a man who was not inclined to minimize difficulty—pleaded earnestly for reinforcement. To no avail.

Once again an American division was to enter the Huertgen Forest assigned a sector too wide for it to cover and given missions far exceeding its capabilities. First it was the 9th Division, then the 9th Division a second time, then the 28th, now the 4th. How long would the procession continue? And through it all, the Roer River Dams and the waters they impounded, whose capture might well have put an end not only to the fighting in the dreaded forest but on the Roer plain as well, remained in German hands, unchallenged, inviolate.

It was not as if higher commanders closed their eyes to the rigors and the cost of the forest fighting. No one regretted any more than did Courtney Hodges of the First Army the mutilation of these fine divisions. Standing one day with his aide beside a road west of the forest, he watched in admiration as survivors of one of the divisions moved back from the front. Turning away, he said softly, "I wish everybody could see them."

But to Courtney Hodges, for all his concern for the men under him, it was also painfully clear that he had a job to do, and, as he saw it, part of that job was conquering the Huertgen Forest. Had anybody been able to tell in advance what incredible advantage the Germans might wring from the forest, perhaps the job might have been done some other way; but by the time the 4th Division entered the woods, Hodges was inextricably committed to the direct course of sweeping the forest, yard by yard. As one of his staff would put it later, "We had a bear by the tail and couldn't turn loose." What was more, it remained incredible to Hodges and his advisors that the Germans with their limited resources could continue to hold in the forest. Each time a new, fresh division attacked, Hodges was confident it was the one that would succeed.

Nor was it that Hodges was unaware of the problems of fighting in the forest. He himself had fought in the Argonne Forest during World War I as a machine-gun company commander and thus knew something of what it was like down where they do the dying. From his headquarters in the same building in the Belgian resort of Spa occupied in World War I by Hindenburg, Hodges was a frequent visitor to the front but usually no farther forward than division command posts. This was unfortunate, for division staffs themselves found it difficult to comprehend fully how completely inhuman, how intolerably miserable were the conditions in the forest.

The fact was, few officers above regimental level could know what it was truly like in the Huertgen Forest. A man had to live in the midst of this kind of fighting, and participate in it fully, to appreciate how men over a period of time could become so completely, so utterly beaten physically and morally that they sometimes even stepped on the bodies of their own dead because they had not the energy to step over.

After a visit to the 4th Division command post on the first day of the November offensive, General Hodges noted that his divisions had been going about the attack in the wrong way. They were "running down roads," he said, rather than "advancing through the woods tightly buttoned up yard by yard."

On the other hand, what choice did a division commander

have when faced with regimental attack zones one, three, five, miles wide? Not excessive in some situations on open ground perhaps, but far too wide for the forest, as already proven by the experiences of the 9th and 28th Divisions. Though the First Army admittedly had a tremendous frontage to cover, considering the troops available and the need to concentrate in order to attack—a frontage so great that all through the fall of 1944 Hodges never could afford the luxury of more than a nominal reserve—the basic fact remained that the divisions in the Huertgen Forest had to bear unreasonable demands.

Because Joe Collins of the VII Corps had specifically ordered "Tubby" Barton to assist the corps main effort by the 1st Division, one regiment of the 4th Division had to attack close alongside the 1st Division's 26th Infantry. Barton gave this assignment to the 8th Infantry under Col. Richard W. McKee. This meant that the other regiment, the 22d Infantry, had to cover the three remaining miles of forest down to the 12th Infantry's positions southwest of Huertgen, a patent impossibility. Lest the two attacking regiments get too far apart, Barton had to risk leaving a big gap between the 22d Infantry and the depleted 12th. Commanded by Col. Charles T. Lanham, the 22d Infantry was to take Kleinhau and Grosshau, two villages astride the main Huertgen–Dueren highway just north of Huertgen.

Despite the limited number of roads in the Huertgen Forest, the 8th Infantry had no real problem. Lanham's 22d Infantry similarly would have adequate roads once the regiment reached the Weisser Weh Creek, but how to get from the line of departure along another creek bed, the Rother Weh, almost a mile west of the Weisser Weh? Nothing but firebreaks ran from one creek to the other across the wooded high ground in between called Raven's Hedge Ridge (*Rabenheck*). Colonel Lanham could bank only on improving a firebreak until the fighting passed beyond the Weisser Weh, whereupon his supply columns might proceed into the 8th Infantry's sector, then south along the Weisser Weh road.

Because engineers manning roadblocks in the forest had

had little enemy contact, the 4th Division gained only meager intelligence information from them. It was clear nevertheless that the enemy was the same nondescript *275th Infantry Division* that had been fighting here since early October.

The only reserve available in Straube's *74th Corps* was what was left of the *116th Panzer Division*. The panzer division already was engaged trying to dislodge the 12th Infantry southwest of Huertgen, and Field Marshal Model at *Army Group B* was making increasingly loud demands that this division be released for refitting for the counteroffensive.

For all the problems facing the Germans, General Barton and his 4th Division could not fail to note that the same ersatz *275th Division* had demonstrated twice already that within the Huertgen Forest a conglomerate force might do the work of a more elite unit. Once the limited network of firebreaks, trails, and roads had been thickly mined and blocked with trees, a few poorly coordinated squads in well-prepared positions might hold off a company or a battalion. Sometimes mud might deny the roads even after the defenders had failed to. Not to mention the fact that American superiority in tanks and artillery brought little advantage in the forest.

So aware of the latter fact was General Barton that he eschewed any artillery preparation before the attack in the somewhat faint hope of gaining surprise. At midday on November 16, while the bombs and big guns pounded other parts of the front, the 4th Division moved silently to the attack.

Climbing a precipitous east bank of the Wehe Creek valley along a firebreak a few yards south of Schevenhuette, the leading battalion of the 8th Infantry came quickly under heavy fire. Machine guns behind a pyramid of three concertinas of barbed wire eight to ten feet high raked every inch of the ground. A thick carpet of lethal wooden and plastic antipersonnel *Schuh* mines also barred the way.

Inching forward on their bellies, a small group of daring men tried to slide a Bangalore torpedo beneath the concertinas. As German fire cut down one man, another took his place. At long last, the explosive finally in position, the men ignited the primer cord and dashed to the rear. The rest of the battalion poised, awaiting the explosion as a signal to rush through the wire.

The cue never came.

The Bangalore torpedo was wet. It did not go off.

During the night, the battalion's Ammunition and Pioneer Platoon succeeded in blowing a gap in the wire, but as daylight came on November 17, the German machine guns thwarted every effort to push through. Three times the men tried it. Three times the Germans drove them back with heavy losses. By noon the battalion's casualties totaled a depressing 200.

In the hope that the Germans could not so adequately cover two gaps, a young platoon leader, 1st Lt. Bernard J. Ray, volunteered to blow a second gap in the wire. Detonator caps in his pocket, a length of primer cord about his body, he crawled forward alone, dragging a Bangalore torpedo beside him. As he reached the wire and began to prepare the torpedo for firing, a shell from a German mortar wounded him severely. Lieutenant Ray's next move was one of those inexplicably heroic things men sometimes do under the stress of combat. Pulling a detonator cap from his pocket, he fitted it to the primer cord about his body, then the primer cord to the Bangalore torpedo.

Having wired himself into the explosive charge, Lieutenant Ray calmly set it off.

A great gap appeared in the wire.

Still the men of the 8th Infantry could not get past.

In the meantime, a mile to the southwest, the 22d Infantry also had attacked at 12:45 the afternoon of the sixteenth. After having made some encouraging early gains against the outposts on Raven's Hedge Ridge, they were stopped by heavy German shelling and by the difficulties involved in trying to turn a firebreak into a route of supply. In three days incredibly accurate German guns killed or wounded all battalion commanders in this regiment, the bulk of the staff officers in two battalions, almost half the company commanders, and many key company officers and noncommissioned officers. Even in view of the heavy casualties normally to be expected among leaders in the close combat of the Huertgen Forest, losing so many key men so quickly bordered on the uncanny.

As for turning the firebreak into a supply route, one complication piled upon another. When a platoon of light tanks inched up the firebreak to help the infantry, the first two tanks set off antitank mines, blocking passage of the others. Though engineers removed the tanks and set out to improve the trail, so sodden was the ground that the passage of only a few vehicles quickly created a quagmire. The Germans in some instances had stacked one antitank mine atop another like pancakes. Often they had fitted them with anti-lifting devices so that the engineers had to explode the mines in place, then fill the craters with soil too soggy to support the weight of trucks. Wheels of vehicles digging deep in muddy ruts sometimes exploded mines missed by mechanical mine detectors.

Despite the casualties and the supply problem, two battalions of the 22d Infantry suddenly strode forward with a rush on the third day, November 18. Having at last found a hole in the German positions, they took the icy Weisser Weh at a run and, as dusk fell, dug in on the first high ground beyond the creek along both sides of the road leading east toward Kleinhau and Grosshau.

At the same time, the commander of the 8th Infantry, Colonel McKee, had decided that no matter how great the problems of mines and rough terrain, tanks and tank destroyers were the only hope for getting past the pyramid of concertina wire. Early on the eighteenth, he sent a platoon each of light and medium tanks to help a fresh infantry battalion past the obstacle.

As the big vehicles lumbered slowly up the firebreak, the infantry followed closely, stepping in the path of the treads for protection against antipersonnel mines. Remarkably, the tanks hit no antitank mines, and such a hail of machine-gun and cannon fire did they maintain that the Germans had no chance to fire a *Panzerfaust*. With a rush the tanks trampled the concertina obstacle. The infantrymen poured through, and in a matter of minutes made quick work of a disheartened group of Germans, then pushed on a full mile into the forest. As everybody who had tried to use tanks in the forest had discovered, the results were almost always worth the risk and the effort.

If the 8th and 22d Regiments had renewed their attacks early on the fourth day, November 19, they would have had an excellent chance of penetrating all the way through the Huertgen Forest, for the *275th Division* had almost run out of men to stop them. Hans Schmidt himself was wounded, though he stayed on the job as division commander. Nor did Straube at the headquarters of the *74th Corps* have any help to send, for what was left of the *116th Panzer Division* at last had to pull out for refitting.

The *Seventh Army's* General Brandenberger had the same problem. Ever since the 4th Division's attack had begun, Erich Brandenberger had been engaged in an almost frantic search for reserves. By stretching defensive lines perilously thin, Brandenberger had finally managed to release from a corps to the south a weak infantry division, the *344th*. Impending arrival of a *volksgrenadier* division scheduled for the counteroffensive also promised release of a second infantry division, the *353d*. But even first contingents of the *344th* could not reach the Huertgen Forest until after nightfall on the nineteenth.

If the 8th and 22d Regiments attacked with vigor during the day of the nineteenth, they obviously could push right through.

This Colonel McKee, Colonel Lanham, and General Barton did not know. Lanham, particularly, was concerned. A thin man with dark, profound eyes hiding behind spectacles, "Buck" Lanham seemed to at least one of his associates to be a man with "a touch of the poet." A friend of the novelist Ernest Hemingway—who himself was present as an observer in the Huertgen Forest—Lanham was a capable but excitable commander. He worried now about the lack of a supply route over Raven's Hedge Ridge. Even had a road been open as far as the Weisser Weh, he still would have been unable to get vehicles across the creek, for the Germans had demolished a bridge and kept the site under uncannily accurate shellfire. Lanham worried too about a south flank exposed for more than two miles, with even the closest troops of the 8th Infantry to the north a mile away. A mile was an alarming distance in the forest.

During the night of the eighteenth, Buck Lanham asked Barton for a twenty-four-hour delay in the attack.

In granting approval, Barton also had to stop the 8th Infantry, lest McKee's regiment get too far forward in the forest for the two regiments to cover each other. He told McKee to spend the period clearing the banks of the Weisser Weh south to the regimental boundary while Lanham did the same in the north. The valley swept of Germans, the 22d Infantry finally would have an adequate, though circuitous, supply route around Raven's Hedge Ridge.

This the two regiments basically had accomplished by nightfall on November 19, but German shellfire at the bridge site on the Weisser Weh continued to prevent engineers from rebuilding the bridge. The engineers were convinced the Germans had left an artillery observer hidden in the woods. Thus the supply situation in the 22d Infantry remained precarious even as both regiments renewed their attacks to the east the next day, November 20.

Though unaware that German reinforcements in the form of the *344th Infantry Division* had been moving into the forest during the night, both regiments found it out soon enough after daylight on the twentieth. In the north, the 8th Infantry registered almost no gain, and when night came again, so closely locked were the opposing forces that German fire prevented the men from cutting logs for overhead cover on their foxholes.

Though the 22d Infantry gained a few hundred yards in the direction of Kleinhau and Grosshau, the Germans fought with determination and launched one small counterattack after another against the regiment's exposed right flank. Casualties soared, even among the reserve battalion, which was fully occupied even though not actually committed in the forward line. This battalion had to protect the open south flank; eliminate German patrols and bypassed strongpoints, including one which took the regimental headquarters under fire; patrol the Weisser Weh road to keep it open; and comb the woods near the bridge site in search of the German suspected of calling down such accurate artillery fire.

Engineers finally circumvented the German shelling by

building a bridge in sections within the woods away from the bridge site. They put it into place the night of the twentieth, but not until the next day did patrols at last uncover the mystery of the accurate shelling. They found an artillery observer, a German officer, hidden with a radio in the woods.

By nightfall on November 20, the 4th Division's two regiments in their five-day attack had achieved no penetration deeper than a mile beyond the Weisser Weh, yet the regiments had already paid an awful price in casualties. Some rifle companies were down below fifty men actually on the firing line, less than 30 per cent of normal strength. Out of the usual six officers, only one or two remained in most companies. For the two regiments the toll in battle losses alone was about 1,500 men, while half a thousand more had succumbed to battle fatigue, trench foot, and other nonbattle ailments. Although replacements had begun what was to become a daily trek to the front lines, they never were to equal the fallen in numbers, and days and weeks would pass before they might approach the fallen in experience. Faces freshly shaved, uniforms free of mud, they made a sharp contrast to the grimy, bearded veterans of the forest fight.

Again the division commander, General Barton, approved a pause. Take another twenty-four hours, Barton said, and get organized for a big push on the twenty-second. There would be hope then, Barton revealed, for eliminating the great gaps between regiments and on the right flank of the division; for the day before, on the nineteenth, the First Army's General Hodges had ordered a change in plan. The change would reduce the 4th Division's responsibilities and at the same time release the battered 12th Infantry for use with the rest of the division.

Still leaning on the hope that one more push, one more division might break the impasse, Hodges on November 19 had ordered another fresh division into the crucible of the Huertgen Forest.

THE VILLAGE OF HUERTGEN

15 By NOVEMBER 19, the failure of the big air and
artillery preparation to precipitate a breakthrough on the VII
Corps front had become all too apparent. The 104th Division
was still fighting to get out of the Stolberg Corridor; the 1st
Division had yet taken only one portion (Hill 232) of the
Hamich Ridge; and the 4th Division was having the usual grim
time of it in the Huertgen Forest.

If General Collins was to achieve a genuine penetration,
the VII Corps obviously needed extra weight. Yet nowhere
within the VII Corps zone had gains been sufficient to make
room for a new force. As General Hodges studied his operations map, the only spot for committing additional strength
appeared to be in the Huertgen Forest. If only the village of
Huertgen could be taken, the 4th Division might break out of
the forest and gain the roadnet leading through relatively open
country to Dueren.

Already Hodges had the force at hand that might do the
job—Combat Command R of the 5th Armored Division. But by
November 19 it had at last become apparent to everyone that
the 12th Infantry would be unable to clear a road to enable the
armor to strike at Huertgen.

To Leonard Gerow and the V Corps Hodges turned again.
Already General Gerow was in the process of relieving the

shattered 28th Division with a fresh force, the 8th Infantry Division. One regiment still had not arrived. Hodges told Gerow to speed the movement of the regiment, relieve the 12th Infantry with it, and attack on November 21 to take both Huertgen and Kleinhau.

Cruel and unmitigating were the demands of the Huertgen Forest, so cruel and unmitigating that any division that fought there was bound to get hurt. Yet not once in the forest fighting had any division commander been accorded a genuine opportunity to overcome the particular problems of the forest fighting without the restrictions of various subsidiary requirements or objectives. In addition to penetrating the forest, the 9th Division in its first attack had been required to take the Hoefen–Alzen Ridge and assist the 3d Armored Division through the Stolberg Corridor. In its second attack, the 9th Division had been forced to hold out one regiment to defend Schevenhuette. The 28th Division had been obligated to gain a line of departure overlooking Huertgen. The 4th Division had had to tie up one regiment on the same assignment.

It was high time somebody realized that conquering the Huertgen Forest was a job enough in itself. Yet again a new division was to enter the forest with much the same kind of predesignated restrictions. Because of the assignment to relieve the 28th Division, at least two regiments of the 8th Division would be required on defensive missions around Simonskall, Raffelsbrand, and Vossenack. This left only one regiment, the 121st Infantry, for opening a road to Huertgen. Because of the additional requirement of relieving the 12th Infantry to enable that regiment to move quickly to the aid of the 4th Division, the 121st Infantry had no choice but to drive toward Huertgen in the same old way. And again, just as the 12th Infantry had been rushed into the forest without time for essential reconnaissance, so was the 121st Infantry scheduled to arrive in the dead of night, take over from another unit in close contact with the enemy, then move forward into the unknown the next morning to attack.

When the order arrived late on the nineteenth to move to the Huertgen Forest, the 121st Infantry was in a defensive position 107 road miles away. Not until the next day could relief be accomplished and the regiment begin to march. Half frozen from riding in open trucks and already wary about the forest from the tales they had heard, the men entered the forest just as an impenetrable, clinging darkness descended. Still ahead of them lay a seven-mile march on foot over muddy, rock-strewn roads, trails, and firebreaks. Rain began to fall in sting-ing, wind-blown sheets. Like an unruly accordion the column moved—the men stumbling, slithering, falling one moment, and the next coming up short against the backs or rifles of the marchers in front of them.

Somewhere along the chain of command, some omniscient authority must have heard the curses and protests of other com-manders from the lowest rifle squad on up, for somebody finally agreed to postpone relief of the 12th Infantry until daylight. But the attack was still to begin at 9 A.M. As the word trickled down the miserable column, men pulled off the trail, collapsed on the wet earth, drew their raincoats about them, and tried to sleep.

Dawn came slowly into the forest, as if reluctant to throw light on the stark, sobering tableau that could have been ar-ranged only by the Devil himself. Once magnificent trees now twisted, gashed, broken, limbs and foliage forming a grotesque carpet on the floor of the forest. Some trees, stripped of all foli-age, standing like gaunt, outsized toothpicks. Great jagged chunks of concrete and twisted reinforcing rods that together had been a pillbox. The mutilated carcass of a truck that had hit a mine. Everywhere discarded soldier equipment—gas masks, empty rations containers, helmets, rifles, here a field jacket with a sleeve rent, there a muddy overcoat with an ugly clotted dark stain on it. One man kicked a bloody shoe from his path, then shuddered to see that the shoe still had a foot in it.

At eight o'clock the big guns began to thunder. For an hour they pounded the woods and the village of Huertgen. When nine o'clock came, all three battalions of the 121st Infan-try somehow were lined up behind the foxholes belonging to the men of the 12th Infantry—or what was left of those men. One battalion headed up the valley of the Weisser Weh. Another attacked through the thick of the woods between the valley and the Germeter–Huertgen highway. The third moved astride the highway.

Hardly had the artillery preparation ended when the pattern the ground fighting would assume for the next four days emerged. On the first day, no unit made any appreciable advance, except for one company east of the Germeter–Huertgen highway that gained a meager 500 yards. The woods were as thick as ever with antipersonnel mines, with log bunkers bristling with machine guns and burp guns, with jagged hunks of tree trunks and small mountains of broken branches and foliage that wore a man out climbing through or over. The wounded early began to stream down the steep slopes, here a white-faced man clutching an arm red with blood, there two men with a stretcher bearing a quiet form with one leg missing. Control in the forest remained as difficult as ever. A rifle platoon and half the Weapons Platoon of Company F disappeared into the woods without a trace. As far as the infantry was concerned, American artillery might have been trying to silence the enemy's big guns with peashooters. Not until dusk fell on the first day did the 121st Infantry accomplish even a complete passage of the 12th Infantry's lines.

For three more days the 121st Infantry plodded on, absorbing alarming casualties, and enduring conditions that made men weep, while no battalion gained more than a few hundred yards. On the second day, November 22, the rain came back, mixed at times with snow. Artillery of both the 8th Division and the V Corps fired one mission after another, with little apparent effect on German guns; and again the infantrymen were locked too close in combat for the artillery to have much effect on the forward German positions. On both November 23 —Thanksgiving Day—and November 24, the regimental commander, Col. John R. Jeter, committed light tanks along the firebreaks, but the tanks bogged helplessly in the mud. A platoon of mediums trying to move up the Germeter–Huertgen highway fell quick prey to German guns in Huertgen.

The first thin hope of success came on Thanksgiving Day, with developments on the regiment's left wing. Here men of the 2d Battalion clung precariously to sharply sloping ground a few hundred yards east of the Weisser Weh. On the twenty-second, Company G had moved west of the creek to hit the opposition from the flank, but hardly had the men begun to advance when the lead platoon ran into a minefield. Among the casualties was the platoon leader, who had both legs blown off. The next day the company tried again, this time sending one platoon on a wider, deeper maneuver. Slipping stealthily through the forest, this platoon made it to the creek and waded across. Pulling themselves up the steep east slope by tugging at trees and bushes, the men gained a hold on the road that twists and turns along the east bank and eventually leads to Huertgen. The platoon was well in rear of a roadblock that had stymied all efforts of the 12th Infantry to open the road for CCR's tanks.

Reacting quickly to the news, the Company G commander, Capt. Walter Black, a tall, blonde young officer, hurried up the road with the rest of his company to try to break through to the platoon. They had not a chance. Because the roadblock was located in a sharp defile, machine guns caught Black and his men with no cover except the ditches on either side of the road. These were alive with antipersonnel mines. One after another the mines went off, and German mortar and artillery fire began to fall. Black and his men had no choice but to fall back, leaving behind a score of dead in the ditches. A platoon leader and Black himself, both veterans of long months of fighting, were so unnerved by the experience that they broke. "They just went berserk," a sergeant said, "crying and yelling."

Obviously unable to reach the platoon beyond the roadblock, the battalion commander that night authorized the men to withdraw. Upset by this failure to exploit the gain, the regimental commander, Colonel Jeter, relieved the battalion commander.

This was the first in what turned out to be a wave of summary reliefs that were touched off by the inconclusiveness of the 121st Infantry's advance. In four days three company commanders lost their commands. In one company all officers either were relieved of their command or broke under the strain. One platoon leader who refused to order his men back into the line was placed under arrest. Jeter also replaced a second battalion commander. General Hodges himself came to the division command post, where he "made it quite clear" to the 8th Division commander that he "expected better results."

This was a military euphemism for "Get cracking, or else."

Through it all, the misery and incredible difficulty of the forest fighting persisted. It was attrition unrelieved. So heavy were overcoats from rain and mud that men bowed under their weight. The rain and constant moisture ate insidiously at radios and weapons. Despite the best efforts of graves registration units, bodies of the dead still lay about in grotesque positions, weather-soaked, the stench from them cloying, depressing. And everywhere mines, a plethora of mines. A man might blunder into a minefield, step on a mine, then in his agony thrash about and set off others that eventually killed him. Worst of all was the diabolical "Bouncing Betty," a three-pronged evil that leaped out of the ground and exploded in the air, likely as not to catch a man between the legs and rip out his sexual organs. The parade of men wounded by mines was constant and demoralizing, so that the thought of stepping on a mine—particularly a "Bouncing Betty"—was with a man at every turn. If not mines, then mortar or artillery shells dropping unheralded from the sky to crack with ear-splitting noise in the treetops and bathe the forest with fiery, jagged metal.

By nightfall on November 24, the 121st Infantry had incurred 600 battle casualties, while an almost equal number of men had been evacuated for other reasons. Yet the woods line overlooking Huertgen remained out of reach.

So optimistic about committing a fresh regiment had been the First Army's General Hodges that he earlier had directed the 5th Armored Division's CCR to pass through to take Huertgen on the second day. Though this had proved flatly impossible, pressure to get the armor into the fight continued. The advance in the valley of the Weisser Weh had been so limited that no hope existed for using the armor there; the only possibility was the Germeter–Huertgen highway. Here a lone infantry company had finally gained the woods line east of the highway, but the Germans still held the woods west of the road, and their guns in Huertgen could pinpoint anything that moved on the highway.

For all the perils, the 8th Division commander, Maj. Gen. Donald Stroh, saw CCR's tanks as the only hope of taking pressure off the infantry and opening a way to Huertgen. He told the CCR commander, Col. Glen H. Anderson, to attack up the Germeter–Huertgen highway before dawn on November 25.

Colonel Anderson was wary. He pointed to two particular problems that would have to be solved if his tanks were to entertain any hope of success, and even then he considered it risky. The Germans would have to be cleared from the woods bordering both sides of the highway, or a well-placed shot from a *Panzerfaust* might spoil the whole effort. Most important of all, a mammoth bomb crater blocking the road above Wittscheidt would have to be filled or bridged, for the woods on either side of the road would prevent the tanks from by-passing the crater.

The 8th Division's operations officer assured him that both these obstacles would be eliminated before daybreak.

As the first light of dawn appeared, the lead tanks of CCR's 10th Tank Battalion reached the crater. To the consternation of the crewmen, they found no fill, no bridge, and no path around the crater.

Not easily discouraged, the commander of the first tank, 1st Lt. J. A. Macaulay, determined to get across anyway.

"I'm going to try to jump the damned thing," he radioed back.

Gathering speed, Macauley's tank roared up the road. At the last moment, the driver applied one final burst of speed.

It was not enough.

The tank slammed into the far wall of the crater, rolled to one side, and lay there, helpless, motor racing, one track spinning.

The noise set off a storm of German mortar and artillery fire that plastered the road and small-arms fire that crackled from the woods to the west. If the men of the 121st Infantry had cleared this part of the woods, then the Germans had come back. Though Colonel Anderson ordered his armored infantry battalion to clear the woods, the going was slow. In less than an hour, one company suffered over sixty casualties, including all its platoon sergeants and platoon leaders.

Everybody worked to try to get the armor moving. Artillery and tank destroyers rained shells into the German lines, while a break in the weather allowed fighter-bombers to bomb and strafe Huertgen. Chemical mortars threw up a smoke screen to give the engineers another try at bridging the crater.

It was late morning when the engineers at last got a bridge in. As a tank commanded by Sgt. William Hurley rattled across, hopes rose anew for victory at Huertgen. But Hurley's tank had proceeded scarcely seventy-five yards when it hit a mine. The disabled tank blocked passage as effectively as had the crater. Though a tank retriever nosed Hurley's tank aside, a round from a German assault gun promptly knocked out the retriever.

Again the road was blocked.

This marked the end of CCR's abortive attempt to move up the Germeter–Huertgen highway. It marked, too, the end of Colonel Jeter's command of the 121st Infantry. In midafternoon General Stroh relieved him, sending to take his place the 8th Division Chief of Staff, Col. Thomas J. Cross. It marked the end also of CCR's participation in the Huertgen fight, for the word now was that the 121st Infantry had to take not only the woods line overlooking Huertgen but the village itself.

Like automatons, the men of the 121st Infantry rose again from their foxholes on the morning of November 26 to get on with the job. Unknown to them, their progress now would be materially affected by events that had been taking place elsewhere in the Huertgen Forest, a few miles to the north in the zone of the 4th Division.

Ostensibly taking a day of rest on November 21 while the 8th Division's 121st Infantry released the 12th Infantry for use in the 4th Division's attack, men of the 8th and 22d Regiments actually were busy enough warding off German patrols, dodging mortar and artillery fire, absorbing replacements, and getting a supply route functioning to Buck Lanham's 22d Infantry. Hope for a quick penetration of the forest still was meager, for neither regiment had advanced much more than a mile beyond the Weisser Weh, and the far edge of the forest was as much as two and a half miles away. Because of the problems experienced in relief, the battered 12th Infantry would be unable for another twenty-four hours to launch an attack to secure the 22d Infantry's dangling right flank.

On the other hand, the very fact of a road open to the 22d Infantry was a big achievement. Also, the two regiments had now closed the gap between them. Encouraged by these developments and convinced that the Germans, despite the arrival of their *344th Division,* could not be strong everywhere in the forest, the two regimental commanders devised maneuvers aimed at finding holes in the German lines. One battalion of each regiment feigned attack with every available weapon, while the other battalion tried to slip around the enemy's flank.

The Germans could not have co-operated more wholeheartedly had they been trying to help. At the demonstrating battalions, relatively secure in log-covered holes, they directed round after round of shellfire. At the other battalions, slipping quietly through the woods, they fired hardly a shot.

On the left, the flanking battalion of the 8th Infantry swept half a mile to the grounds of a ruined monastery. Only here did the Germans muster a fight. While this engagement developed, the regimental commander, Colonel McKee, sent his reserve battalion through the same hole the other had discovered, then bypassed the monastery. On the next day—Thanksgiving—and the day after that, the 8th Infantry continued to advance by short bounds, so that by nightfall on November 24 the regiment stood just under a mile from the edge of the forest.

Buck Lanham's 22d Infantry achieved an even more spectacular gain at first. The battalion stealing around the enemy's flank met not a suggestion of opposition. Alongside a creek and then along firebreaks, the battalion slipped like a phantom through the thick forest. The first day, November 22, the men marched more than a mile, and at nightfall they dug in astride a juncture of dirt roads less than a quarter of a mile from the fringe of the forest and the long-sought objective, the village of Grosshau.

The problem was, how to supply this battalion and to get tanks or tank destroyers forward to support an assault on Grosshau until the bypassed Germans along the main road could be eliminated. This took time, as did the maneuver of the 12th Infantry, hastily shored up with replacements, to sweep the forest along Colonel Lanham's south flank.

The 12th Infantry still was a day short of providing full security on the flank, but the main road to the battalion west of Grosshau was open, when Colonel Lanham late on the twenty-fourth learned of the attempt to be made the next day against Huertgen by the 5th Armored Division's CCR. Hoping to gain some advantage by attacking at the same time as the combat command, Lanham ordered two battalions to move against Grosshau.

His battalions seriously understrength, Lanham depended heavily at Grosshau on surprise and the weight of tanks and tank destroyers. He gained neither. It took all morning for the big vehicles to pick their way over muddy trails and firebreaks, and the noise of their movement usurped every vestige of surprise. By the time the jump-off finally came at noon, CCR's drive on Huertgen had failed. German gunners in Grosshau made quick work of the supporting weapons, while violent concentrations of artillery and mortar fire drove the infantry just as quickly back into the forest.

This failure presented "Tubby" Barton, the 4th Division commander, with another all too vivid reminder of the condition of his regiments. The 22d Infantry had reached the edge of the forest; the 12th Infantry could be expected to come abreast of the 22d in another day; and the 8th Infantry had just under a mile to go; but how to achieve the extra push for the final surge?

The 4th Division obviously was close to exhaustion. Because its leaders had to move about to encourage the men under them, they had been among the first to fall. Seasoned junior leaders—squad and platoon sergeants, lieutenants, and company commanders—had almost ceased to exist. An apprehensive parade of replacements kept the battalions at presentable strength, but the new men, no matter how willing, simply did not have the ability of the veterans they replaced. Great stretches of the roads, trails, and firebreaks still were infested with mines, and vehicles traveling routes the engineers deemed clear might still set off an explosion. Company K lost three cooks and its Thanksgiving dinner that way. Mud remained a problem too, for every day since the twentieth had brought some measure of snow, sleet, or rain. Carrying parties under constant threat of enemy shelling or patrols had to lug food, ammunition, or casualties over distances as great as a mile. And again a big gap had grown between the 8th and 22d Regiments.

As night came on November 25, General Barton decided once more to pause. Again the two forward regiments were to consolidate while the 12th Infantry, having eliminated the threat to Colonel Lanham's south flank, pulled back to move in between the other two.

That the 12th Infantry, so recently shattered in the meat-grinder fighting southwest of Huertgen, would now be available for a new assignment after having secured the 4th Division's right flank, was one of the most striking anomalies of all the Huertgen Forest campaign. Given less than twenty-four hours after the earlier debacle to reorganize and bring line companies up to an average strength of about a hundred men, the 12th Infantry had circled far around to the west, then attacked again to reach the woods line west of Huertgen. The goal was only a few hundred yards away from the other stretch of woods line southwest of the village for which the regiment had battled so futilely just a short time before.

Despite intense mortar and artillery fire, it took less than three days to do the job. By mid-morning on November 25— the day the 5th Armored's CCR tried to reach Huertgen— Company G, 12th Infantry, had slipped in behind the last defenders in this part of the forest and staked claim to the woods line.

Incredible it was to these men to sit now almost within

spitting distance of the same ground for which they had fought and bled in vain for a fortnight. Incredible it was too that somebody had not before tried a deep envelopment to outflank the determined Germans southwest of Huertgen. For this was, in effect, what Company G and the rest of the 12th Infantry had now accomplished.

Anybody in the 121st Infantry who had dared predict that a renewed attack on November 26 in the bloody, mutilated woods southwest of Huertgen would sweep rapidly to the woods line overlooking the village would have been hustled off to the medics as an obvious victim of combat fatigue.

Yet that was how it was.

Constant pressure by the 121st Infantry over five days, plus the threat posed by the 4th Division's 12th Infantry west of Huertgen, finally did it. The last of Schmidt's *275th Division* pulled back, leaving only stragglers and a generally irresolute rear guard. Still bothered by occasional shelling and by the ubiquitous mines, men of the 2d Battalion pushed up the trail from the Weisser Weh and an hour before noon reached the woods line.

A kind of jubilation—half disbelief, half relief—swept through the exhausted regiment and up the chain of command.

The assistant 8th Division commander, Brig. Gen. Charles A. Canham, hurried to the forward positions. Air observers, he said, had spotted a column marching away from Huertgen. The Germans, he insisted, had abandoned the village. The new 121st Infantry commander, Colonel Cross, ordered an immediate attack to take the objective that had by now become a kind of symbol of all the dread, misery, death, and frustration of the forest fighting.

It was a hasty, ill-supported attack that sent Company F hurrying across the 800 yards of open ground toward the village. Hardly had the men come full into the open when small-arms fire and shelling sent them scurrying back toward the woods line. The withdrawal report, Company F would attest, was grossly exaggerated.

Through the night Colonel Cross readied a new attack

to hit Huertgen at dawn the next morning, November 27. A calm, steady commander, a firm believer in maneuver, Tom Cross obtained use of a battalion of the 13th Infantry that had been released in a shuffle of defensive positions elsewhere in the 8th Division. Commanded by Lt. Col. Morris J. Keesee, this battalion was to circle far around behind troops of the 4th Division to come upon Huertgen from the northwest and cut the highway leading out of the village. In the meantime, the 2d Battalion, 121st Infantry, was to renew the drive from the woods line southwest of Huertgen.

Neither of the two company commanders scheduled to lead the 2d Battalion's attack was happy with the plan for artillery support. Both 1st Lt. Paul Boesch of Company G, a big, affable man with the cauliflower ears of a wrestler and one of the thickest, blackest beards in all of the Huertgen Forest, and Capt. John R. Cliett of Company F, a tall, heavy-set youngster with a thick Southern accent, protested the plan. The two company commanders wanted permission for Company F to pull back a safe distance from the first houses in Huertgen to enable the artillery to include these houses in the preattack preparation. But nobody in authority would authorize the slightest withdrawal. Too many heads in the 121st Infantry already had rolled.

Traces of daylight were appearing across the tops of the buildings when the thin olive-drab line that was Companies F and G began to move. Even the artillery fire that was pummeling the center of Huertgen ceased. "It was almost," Boesch recalled later, "as if the silence itself had exploded." The men felt "frightened, naked, alone."

Here and there German gunners in half a dozen different houses along the fringe of the village fired nervous bursts with machine guns and burp guns. Arcs of fiery tracer bullets played with deadly grace across the fields.

As it grew lighter, German fire increased in volume and accuracy. Men of one platoon of Company F got into one house, there to fight alone through much of the day, out of touch with anybody to the rear. The bulk of these men died in the fight; the others, when their ammunition gave out, surrendered. The rest of Company F meanwhile fell back to the woods.

Lieutenant Boesch and Company G—some sixty men— made it as far as a communications trench a hundred yards short of the first houses, where they crouched for the rest of the day, powerless to move forward or back; for every time a man stuck his head above the lip of the trench, German fire cut him down as if with a scythe. A growing number of wounded men accumulated in a little covered dugout at one end of the trench.

"Lieutenant," the wounded would say, "when are you going to get us out of here?"

Nobody in the rear did much to help. Artillery continued to fire from time to time, and fighter-bombers took advantage of the brightest day since the 8th Division had come into the Huertgen Forest to bomb and strafe the village; but without a co-ordinated plan of attack, this accomplished little. At one point tank destroyers took the troublesome first houses under fire and Boesch tried to follow up with an assault, but the German machine guns chattered with the same maddening persistence as before.

As night came, Boesch got the wounded out and the food forward, but the only instructions from his battalion commander were to move into Huertgen, since the Germans apparently had abandoned the village. Colonel Keesee's battalion of the 13th Infantry, the word was, had already reached the center of the village from the other end.

Boesch had no way of knowing this was erroneous. Actually, Keesee's men had cut the highway north of Huertgen and had sent a patrol to the center of the village, but that was all. What Boesch did know was that every time his men tried to advance, German fire cut them down. Under these circumstances, he could not accept the thesis that the Germans had abandoned Huertgen. Yet it was hard to argue with rank. Only by sending first one patrol, then another, into Huertgen to see if the Germans had left did Boesch manage to stall through the night.

It was mid-morning when the lieutenant and his little

band of Company G heard the roar of tank motors from the forest to the rear. As the tanks raced into the open, their big cannon began to throw round after round into Huertgen. Little dots—infantrymen of Companies E and F—hurried forward with them. "Get set to move!" Boesch yelled at his men. "Pass the word along. Get set to go with the tanks!"

As the tanks came abreast of them, the men of Company G joined the attack. Within minutes they were inside the first houses, rooting cowed Germans from lower floors and cellars.

The moving spirit behind this attack was a colonel who believed in being up where the shooting was. This was Col. P. D. Ginder, an officer assigned temporarily to the 8th Division because his own division was overstrength in colonels. Sent to Huertgen to get the attack moving, Ginder did just that.

"If you get wounded," Ginder told one officer, "you'll get a nice rest in the hospital. If you get killed, you won't know anything more about it. If neither happens, you have nothing to worry about. Let's get going!"

It was a wild, terrible, awe-inspiring thing, Paul Boesch recalled later, the sweep through Huertgen. Never had Boesch considered that battle could be so incredibly impressive— awful, horrible, deadly, yet somehow thrilling, exhilarating. Everywhere the firecracker sound of small-arms fire, the boom of big guns, the sharp, ear-splintering explosion of shells. Walls and whole buildings collapsed, spraying the landscape with dust, brick, mortar, flame, and smoke. Behind hand grenades heaved through doors and windows, riflemen charged into the buildings. Tanks churned and clattered. Everywhere the smell of burning things—wood, straw, gunpowder, flesh—an acrid, choking, nose-pinching smell. Here and there, dead of both sides. From the new-dead, blood still flowing.

By nightfall on November 28, the 121st Infantry could report that the village of Huertgen, the elusive objective for which so many had died, at last was in hand. The scores of dead Germans and over 200 prisoners attested to the fact that the enemy had not, as many on the American side had argued, abandoned the village, even after Colonel Keesee's battalion of the 13th Infantry cut the road on the far edge.

The Germans had fought for Huertgen to the last and in the process had seen to it that the little farming community would long bear the terrible scars of battle.

THE "BIG RED ONE" IN THE FOREST

16 No U.S. DIVISION in World War II had higher *esprit de corps* than did the "Big Red One." Just being a part of the 1st Division appeared to exert a special influence on a man. It affected commanders, too. Early in the war, in Sicily, so high was the *esprit* and so strong the personal loyalty to the division commander that it hindered the working of the division with other units; the result was that both commanding general and assistant division commander had to be relieved. That was when Ralph Huebner, an iron disciplinarian, was chosen to take over.

By November 1944 being a part of the 1st Division seemed to the VII Corps commander, Joe Collins, to have affected even the steel-willed Ralph Huebner. To Collins, Huebner appeared to be protecting the division, commendably trying to hold down casualties but in the process failing to push hard enough.

This was in Collins' mind when on November 19 he went to Huebner's command post. In three days' fighting, the 1st Division, making the corps' main effort, had taken only Hamich and Hill 232 and made inconclusive gains in the Huertgen Forest. Collins in typical fashion spared no words in letting Huebner know how thoroughly dissatisfied he was.

With the counterattacks of the *47th Volks Grenadier Division* fresh in mind, General Huebner said something about holding the enemy in check.

This was unfortunate. Collins pounced on it.

"Holding the enemy in check!" he thundered. "I knew you could do *that*. I want you to advance. This is an offensive!"

The chastened Huebner revised his plan of attack. Shifting the 16th Infantry away from the Wehe Creek valley to serve as a bridge to the 104th Division farther north, he sent his reserve regiment, the 18th Infantry, along both sides of the Wehe Creek valley toward Langerwehe, the portal to the Roer Plain. This had the virtue of putting on one unit the responsibility for opening the highway alongside the creek.

A battalion of the 18th Infantry gained a leg on the renewed offensive late in the afternoon of November 19. Catching the Germans of the *47th Volks Grenadier Division* temporarily off balance in the wake of the defeats at Hamich and Hill 232, the battalion moved a mile northeast to the village of Wenau, a third of the distance to Langerwehe.

Perched in a commanding position on the left shoulder of the valley, Wenau controlled a major segment of the highway alongside the creek. Its capture provided a promise of early use of the highway to replace the muddy firebreaks that heretofore had served the 26th Infantry in the woods. With this in mind, the regimental commander, Colonel Seitz, decided to renew his drive on the Laufenburg and the wooded hills around the castle early on the twentieth.

Though the 26th Infantry first had to beat off another counterattack by a battalion of the *47th Volks Grenadier Division*, the result was a speedier advance on the castle. Aping the tactic he had used so successfully the day before, Seitz sent a battalion close on the enemy's heels once the Germans began to fall back.

By nightfall on November 20, the Laufenburg and the hills around it were in hand. Then for two more days, through November 22, the 26th Infantry continued to push slowly through the forest. Though the usual miseries of the forest fighting, including high casualties, were all present, the 26th Infantry as night fell on November 22 had only a few hundred yards to go before emerging from the forest.

Colonel Seitz and his men were soon ready to move out

of the forest, but General Huebner was reluctant to give his approval. Surprisingly, the regiment in the forest had advanced faster than any other contingent of the 1st Division. The position of the 26th Infantry, however, formed a potentially dangerous salient, especially since the 4th Division's 8th Infantry to the south was still lagging far behind, and on this date was no more than a mile past the Weisser Weh. Huebner told Seitz to hold fast until the 18th Infantry astride the Wehe Creek could come abreast.

After a relatively painless conquest of Wenau, the 18th Infantry had run into trouble. During the night of the twentieth, General Bork of the 47th Division hurriedly shored up the next village of Heistern with his division engineer battalion. If the 18th Infantry was to get to Langerwehe and at the same time open the Wehe Creek highway, the regiment had to have Heistern, a village hanging high up the sharp western slope of the valley. Germans in Heistern could deny access to the valley highway simply by rolling hand grenades down the slope.

All day long on November 21 a battalion of the 18th Infantry with the help of a platoon of attached medium tanks fought to get into Heistern. Through it all the men were acutely conscious of German observation from high ground not quite a mile to the northeast, Hill 203, the last height before the ground drops sharply to Langerwehe and the Roer Plain. Not until the coming of dusk cut German vision from Hill 203 did the 18th Infantry get into Heistern in strength, and then into only half the village. The Germans still clung like cockleburrs to the other half.

During the night a regimental commander of the 47th Division, Col. Josef Kimbacher, arrived in Heistern with two companies to reinforce what was left of the garrison. In early morning darkness Kimbacher personally led a counterattack that for a time threatened to throw the men of the 18th Infantry out of the village. Not until the Americans had killed 250 of the Germans and captured 120, including Kimbacher, did the fighting die down.

As daylight came on November 22, the 18th Infantry finished clearing Heistern with comparative ease, but the threat posed by the dominating ground of Hill 203 remained. Pounded by German shells obviously directed from the heights, it took almost two days to get through a patch of woods near the base of the hill. From the edge of these woods, it was clear that an assault up the open slopes of the hill itself could not succeed without help from either fighter-bombers or tanks. Gloomy weather eliminated any hope of an assist from the air, and getting tanks forward in full view of the Argus-eyed Germans on Hill 203 proved a major undertaking.

Hopeful of getting help from a flank, the regimental commander, Col. George A. Smith, sent another battalion across the Wehe Creek valley to seize a wooded hill opposite Hill 203, but even after the hill was taken, the problems of counterattack and infiltration persisted. The same was true on the left flank. Here, while the attached 47th Infantry was fighting doggedly to clear the rest of the Hamich Ridge, the 16th Infantry had plowed slowly northeast through patches of woods near the extremity of the Stolberg Corridor. The regiment was too involved with problems of its own to provide help against Hill 203.

The Germans here for the most part still represented the ill-starred *47th Division*. Yet for all the problems earlier encountered from Allied bombardment this division had fought with grim determination. A "suicidally stubborn unit," the 1st Division would later call it.

By nightfall on November 24, the *47th Division* was running out of men. So depleted was this unit and the adjacent *12th Division* under Gerhard Engel that General Von Zangen at the headquarters of the *Fifteenth Army* (alias *Gruppe von Manteuffel*) ordered the two commands to be combined into a single *Kampfgruppe* (task force) under Engel.

Recognizing this to be no more than a stopgap measure, Zangen begged his superiors for at least one division from the reserve that was forming for the winter counteroffensive. He must have this, Zangen argued, or *Gruppe Engel* might soon collapse, leaving the road to Dueren open.

Though the high command back in Berlin turned down the request flatly, they sugared the pill with word that the

3d Parachute Division was soon to arrive from Holland and might be used to relieve both the *12th* and *47th Volks Grenadier Divisions.* What was left of the *volksgrenadiers* were then to be released for the counteroffensive.

As so often happened in the Huertgen Forest fighting, a new German unit thus was on the way at the precise moment the fighting became critical. On November 24, Joe Collins of the VII Corps constructed a special task force around the 47th Infantry and a medium tank battalion of the 3d Armored Division for the specific purpose of breaking onto the Roer plain and ending the slow, plodding advance through the purlieus of the Huertgen Forest. As this task force began to attack early on the twenty-fifth along the left flank of the 1st Division's 16th Infantry, Colonel Smith's 18th Infantry at last got tanks—albeit only two—to the base of Hill 203 and put one rifle platoon on the crest of the hill. Though a tenuous hold, it denied the Germans much of their previous observation advantage and foreshadowed an early end to the slow push to Langerwehe.

Still on the way from Holland, the *3d Parachute Division* might have been entirely too late had not *Gruppe Engel* mustered one last show of muscle that kept General Collins' armor-reinforced task force off the Roer plain until almost dark on November 26. This enabled the paratroopers to counterattack soon after nightfall to blunt the first move onto the plain.

Like all German parachute units at this stage of the war, the *3d Parachute Division* had no claim to its famous name except as an honorific. The men, most of whom ranged in age from sixteen to nineteen, had had no parachute training and almost as little combat experience; yet when conditions were favorable, they might make up in daring what they lacked in military sophistication.

The conditions at first were none too favorable. The paratroopers were getting set to counterattack at the some moment that the 16th Infantry began an artillery preparation as a prelude to helping reduce Hill 203 and take Langerwehe. At the first burst of American shelling, the inexperienced youngsters dived for cellars and foxholes. Under artillery fire, a veteran subofficer observed caustically, "The iron in the hearts of these kids turns to lead in their pants."

Almost the same thing happened at Hill 203, where a battalion of paratroopers moved to retake the crest. The Germans arrived just as the 18th Infantry began a preparatory barrage to sweep the reverse slope of the hill and carry the regiment into Langerwehe. The disheartened young paratroopers surrendered in bunches.

But not so at every point along the front. Fighting from the protection of houses in Langerwehe, the paratroopers prevented final clearing of the town until late the next day, November 28. With the help of assault guns, they also discouraged further use of the armored task force on the Roer Plain. Not to mention what the paratroopers accomplished at the village of Merode.

To the men of the 26th Infantry, Merode was no ordinary objective. Located two miles southeast of Langerwehe beyond the skirt of the Huertgen Forest, Merode was a promise of no more tree bursts, no more dismal forest. But to fulfill the promise, the regimental commander, Colonel Seitz, would be able to use only one battalion. The other two were already tied up in trying to maintain contact with adjacent units.

Merode sprawls near the base of the slope where the heights of the Huertgen Forest bow to the cleared flatland of the Roer Plain. The infantry was to attack downhill to the village, and the only approach for vehicles was a narrow cart track through the forest. Though this track was difficult for tanks, the infantry battalion commander, Lt. Col. Derrell M. Daniel, believed it could be used. He told an attached platoon of tanks to proceed down the trail once the infantrymen had gained the first houses.

Behind a sharp artillery preparation, Colonel Daniel sent two companies against Merode just before noon on November 29. Though a battalion of paratroopers defended the village, artillery fire and several strikes by tactical aircraft helped the infantrymen into the first houses by mid-afternoon.

As Daniel gave the signal, the platoon of tanks started

forward. Hardly had they left the concealment of the woods when a hail of German artillery and antitank fire pounded the open slope. Two of the tanks made it, though one was quickly knocked out inside the village. Commanders of the other two shied at the fire and turned back. As they backed up, a shell struck a track of the lead tank. The tank overturned. Because of deep cuts, high fills, and dense, stalwart trees on either side of the narrow trail, no vehicle could get past the damaged tank into Merode.

Through the early part of the night, commanders at various echelons tried in various ways to get more tank and antitank support into Merode, but they might have been dogs baying at the moon, so futile were their efforts. The best hope —a tank retriever that was supposed to remove the damaged tank—failed to do the job. Engineers then began building a bypass, which at best would be a long, tedious process.

Nobody apparently realized until too late how desperate the situation was in Merode. Not long before midnight, the Germans boxed in the village with a heavy concentration of shellfire to deny reinforcements. Soon after, they counterattacked. Because continuous use had seriously weakened the batteries of the radios of the two companies in the village, communications failed. No one knew where to direct artillery fire to help stop the German drive.

At long last, a plaintive message, barely audible, came over Colonel Daniel's radio set.

"There's a Tiger tank coming down the street now," the voice said, "firing his gun into every house."

There was a pause.

"He's three houses away now!"

Another pause.

"Here he comes!"

The radio fell silent.

For all practical purposes, this marked the end of the 26th Infantry's fight for Merode. It also marked the end of the 1st Division's role in the battle of the Huertgen Forest. In just over two weeks, the 1st Division and the attached 47th Infantry had registered a total advance of not quite four miles from Schevenhuette to Langerwehe. In view of the opposition, the weather, the forest, and the terrain, this was an impressive accomplishment, but in view of the great expectations that had gone with the division, the result was sobering.

In achieving this small gain, the 1st Division had paid with 4,000 battle casualties, including over 600 in the attached 47th Infantry. The 26th Infantry alone, the regiment that fought fully within the Huertgen Forest, lost 1,479 men, including 163 killed and 261 missing (most of whom were later declared killed). Nonbattle losses attributable to combat exhaustion, trench foot, and the weather raised these figures by at least a third.

Three days after the debacle at Merode, Joe Collins told Ralph Huebner he would ask no more of the 1st Division than straightening the line and consolidating defenses in preparation for relief by a fresh division. As the men of the Big Red One got ready to fall back, the Huertgen Forest lay behind, but the goal of the Roer River was still three miles away.

"ONLY A HANDFUL OF OLD MEN LEFT"

17 WHILE COMMANDING the 8th Division at Brest, Donald Stroh had watched helplessly as a fighter-bomber supporting his division's attack crashed in flames on a Brittany hillside. The pilot, Stroh found out later, was his son.

By November 1944 Stroh was a tired man, his already strained nerves severely tried by the personal tragedy that had struck him. To his superiors, the difficulties experienced by his division's 121st Infantry in trying to take Huertgen reflected in some measure the fatigue of the division commander. To allow General Stroh to return to the United States for rest and recuperation—the way they put it when they wanted to replace a commander without the stigma of summary relief—Courtney Hodges brought in a replacement, an assistant division commander from the Third Army, Brig. Gen. William G. Weaver.

Assured on November 28 that Huertgen would fall, General Stroh said good-bye to his division. General Weaver, who somewhere had picked up the nickname "Wild Bill," took charge.

Weaver promptly called up the 5th Armored Division's CCR to Huertgen. The combat command, Weaver directed, was to attack the next morning to take Kleinhau, a mile northeast of Huertgen.

As good weather continued late on the twenty-eighth,

planes of the Ninth TAC bombarded Kleinhau. The next morning, within minutes after an armored task force left the fringe of Huertgen, tanks were cruising among the buildings of the village. A lone Mark IV tank knocked out one Sherman before the Americans could eliminate it, and an assault gun in woods to the east also scored one hit, but in the main, conquest of Kleinhau was a mopping-up assignment.

With both Huertgen and Kleinhau out of the way, the 8th Division and the attached combat command had completed their Huertgen Forest assignment as originally given by the First Army. It had taken 1,247 casualties—most of them in the 121st Infantry—to do it, an awesome price for such a limited advance, but a price that had become standard in the forest fighting. What was more, the gain bought at such a price meant that the adjacent 4th Division now might flaunt its tail at Kleinhau and swing northeast over fairly open ground toward the Roer at Dueren.

From a cooks' and bakers' school in the United States, Pvt. Morris Sussman was transferred for seventeen weeks' basic infantry training, then shipped overseas. With 200 other men in a "packet" of infantry replacements, Sussman arrived in Scotland in early November, yet by the middle of the month he found himself in the Huertgen Forest.

At Service Company, 22d Infantry, Sussman and his companions spent a cold night sleeping in pup tents and listening in awe to the boom of the artillery. The next day they got in trucks and moved to an infantry battalion headquarters deep in the forest. Here somebody gave them their company assignments and noted their names and serial numbers.

As a guide led them east through the forest, they saw a number of "Jerry" and American dead. Private Sussman said he was "horrified" at the sight of the dead, but not as much as he might have been, "because everything appeared as if it were in a dream."

A first sergeant, taking charge of Sussman and twenty-six other men scheduled to go to Company E, led them to a group of dugouts, where they spent the night. Here Sussman learned for sure he was in E Company and somebody said he was in the First Army. He had no idea what regiment or what division he belonged to.

The next morning the company commander called Sussman over.

"You know how to operate a radio?" the captain asked.

Sussman said, "No, sir."

The captain handed him a radio. "You're going to learn," he said.

Learning, Sussman discovered, consisted of carrying the radio on his back and calling the captain whenever he heard the captain's name over the radio.

Sussman said that when first told he was going to be a radio operator, he felt "good." This meant he would be with the captain, and back in the States he had heard that captains stayed "in the rear." Actually, Sussman said, he and the captain "quite often found themselves out in front of the whole company."

Pvt. Morris Sussman was one of 4,924 replacements absorbed into the 4th Division during the thirty days of November 1944. There was little that was unusual about him, except that he happened to become a radio operator instead of a rifleman. That, plus the fact that he came out of the Huertgen Forest alive and with no wound or purple toes to show for it.

As General Barton on November 25 ordered the 8th and 22d Regiments to consolidate while he moved the 12th Infantry to cover the big gap of uncleared woods between them, these three regiments were, in effect, impostors masquerading under the names of three veteran regiments. In ten days some companies had run through three and four company commanders. Staff sergeants and sergeants commanded almost all rifle platoons. Most squad leaders were inexperienced privates or privates first class. One company that normally would have had 180 men had only twenty-five, including replacements. So unusual was it to get replacements into the line without incurring losses that companies noted with pride when they accomplished it. The front-line stay of some men was so short that when evacuated to aid stations they did not know what platoon, company, battalion, or even regiment they had been serving with.

Under conditions like these, it was axiomatic that men and leaders would make needless mistakes often causing great losses. The fact was, the 4th Division now was less a division than a conglomeration. One man summed it all up in a few words: "Then they jump off again, and soon there is only a handful of the old men left."

This was how it was. Yet a job had to be done, and these were the men who had to do it. General Barton and the regimental commanders issued their orders. Battalion, company, and platoon commanders passed them down the line.

"Well, men," a sergeant said, "we can't do a ——— thing sitting still."

He got out of his hole, took a few steps, and started shooting. His men went with him.

That was how this weary division resumed the attack.

No matter how essential had been the third pause in the 4th Division's operations, it was unfortunate in that once again the delay had given the Germans time to move in new troops. This time it was the *353d Infantry Division* under General Mahlmann, brought up from the *Seventh Army's* south wing, the same division that in September had held this sector briefly before retiring in favor of Schmidt's *275th Division*. The *353d* remained seriously understrength, but the depleted, replacement-studded 4th Division still would feel the new presence sharply.

The critical action developed at Grosshau. Here, where the 22d Infantry had reached the fringe of the forest, General Barton had arranged to use a portion of the 5th Armored Division, Combat Command A, to reinforce his faltering 22d Infantry. But first the infantry had to take Grosshau and a patch of woodland beyond the village in order to secure the highway needed for the armor to drive on Dueren.

The unpleasant memory of the first direct attack against Grosshau fresh in mind, the 22d Infantry commander, Buck Lanham, had devised a new plan. Taking into account the position of Grosshau on the forward slope of a hill, Lanham intended to send a battalion through the woods to the north to come upon the crest from a flank, thus cutting off the village. He hoped also to attack at the same time, early on November 29, that a task force of armor was hitting Kleinhau, less than a mile south of Grosshau.

A battalion started soon after daylight on this maneuver, which took more time than Lanham had figured. It was noon, the Kleinhau attack had already ended, and the division Chief of Staff was pressuring Lanham to get going against Grosshau, and still the flanking battalion had not reached the edge of the woods near the hill. Lanham at last could no longer resist demands from division headquarters that he get an attack underway immediately. He had no choice but another direct assault from the west.

Hardly had the infantrymen left the concealment of the woods when the conscientious Lanham regretted the decision. Mortar, artillery, and machine-gun fire quickly pinned the men to the ground, then worked them over unmercifully.

Here is how a medical aid man in a German company saw it:

The earth trembles; the concussion takes our breath. Two wounded are brought to my hole, one with a torn-up arm, the other with both hands shot off. I am considering whether to cut off the rest of the arm. I'll leave it on. How brave these two are. I hope to God all this is not in vain.

To our left machine guns begin to chatter, and here comes the Ami. In broad waves you can see him come across the field. Tanks all around him are firing wildly. . . . Can't stick my head out of the hole. Finally here are three German assault guns. With a few shots we can see several tanks burning. Long smoke columns are rising. The attack slows. It's stopped.

As night approached, the attack looked like an abject failure from the American viewpoint. Yet Lanham and his men had in reality done more damage to the enemy than they knew. The German aid man described it this way:

Unbelievable with this handful of men [that] we can hold out against such attacks! . . . Our people are dropping like tired flies. If we only had the munitions and the heavy weapons that the American has, he would have gone to the devil a long time ago. But as it is, there is only a silent holding out to the last man.

When the Ami really attacks again, then he has got to break through. I can't believe this land can be held any longer. Many of our boys just ran away; can't find them and have to hold out with this small group. But we are going to fight.

[Then] it starts again. As usual, first the wild artillery . . . then amidst yells they are breaking out of the forest amongst their tanks. Now our weapons begin to speak. The Ami is getting closer now, but the murderous fire of our machine guns forces him to the ground. More tanks are knocked out. When the Ami sees this he turns around and retreats into the forest. But the Americans are insulted. Now he really starts hammering us with his heavy weapons. . . . Suddenly hordes of Amis are breaking out of the forest. Murderous fire meets them, but he does not even take cover any more. We shoot until the barrels sizzle. Hand grenades are bursting, but we cannot hold them any longer. We have got to go back. Already we see brown figures through the trees. I turn around and walk away. Very calmly, with my hands in my pockets. They are not even shooting at me, perhaps because of the red cross on my back.

What the aid man saw was Lanham's flanking battalion at last breaking out of the woods to cut the highway leading north out of Grosshau and emerge on the high ground in the rear of the village. At almost the same moment, in gathering darkness, a covey of tanks and tank destroyers took advantage of the dusk to join the infantry stymied along the road from the west. Firing their guns constantly, the big vehicles raced into the village. Resistance quickly collapsed. By the light of buildings burning with eerie flickers and of a moon that shone for the first time since the 4th Division had entered the Huertgen Forest, the men methodically eliminated the last Germans from the village.

Anxious to get the 5th Armored's CCA moving northeast toward Dueren, General Barton during the night authorized Colonel Lanham to use the combat command's 46th Armored Infantry Battalion to help on November 30 with two tasks that remained to be done before the tanks could roll. One was to occupy Hill 401, a bald knob a few hundred yards beyond Grosshau from which the Germans might bring under fire anything that moved up the main highway. This job Lanham gave to the armored infantry. The other was to clear a patch of woods on either side of the highway leading to the next village of Gey and a straight run to Dueren. The latter assignment Lanham gave his own riflemen.

The job on Hill 401 was not supposed to be difficult. The word was that comrades from CCR already had cleared the hill in the process of taking Kleinhau.

The word was wrong.

As the armored infantrymen marched up the hill, expecting to find friendly outposts at the top, a murderous fire rained down on them. The men had to shift to attack formation in full view of the Germans, then work their way gradually, painfully from one little fold in the ground to another, while German machine guns were chattering. Incredibly, the visiting infantrymen from the 5th Armored Division made it before the day was over, but when night came only half the battalion remained to fight again.

One of Buck Lanham's organic battalions of the 22d Infantry meanwhile advanced behind the fire of fourteen tanks to sweep swiftly through the woods west of the Grosshau–Dueren highway and come to the woods line overlooking Gey. The next day another battalion accomplished the same thing east of the road. At long last, sixteen days after the start of the big November offensive, a regiment of the 4th Division— or what was left of it—was all the way through the Huertgen Forest.

Success, yes; but how to maintain it? Every man of the rifle battalions was in a foxhole somewhere, yet the line was desperately thin. As a last resort, Colonel Lanham built a reserve around men from his Antitank, Headquarters, and Service Companies. The need for a reserve became all too apparent before daylight on December 2. Striking from Gey, the Germans counterattacked. In no greater than company strength, they nevertheless gave every indication of rolling up the feeble 22d Infantry's positions. Only prompt artillery support and hasty commitment of Lanham's tiny reserve saved the day.

Had events proceeded as General Barton had intended, the 5th Armored Division's CCA now would have joined the 22d Infantry and the rest of the 4th Division in the final push across open ground to Dueren. But the 22d Infantry, hard put to hold its own against no more than one enemy company, plainly could not help; the sad fact was that the condition of the 22d Infantry was equally that of the entire 4th Division.

In the center of the division's zone, the newly inserted 12th Infantry had gained the woods line west of Gey late on the last day of November, but this regiment too was nothing but a shell. The 8th Infantry on the division's north wing meanwhile had run into a particularly strong position erected by a regiment of the newly arrived 353d *Division*. Not until late on December 1 was the 8th Infantry able to achieve anything resembling a penetration, and then the companies were too weak to exploit it. No company had as much as a third of its normal strength, and Company I was down to twenty-one men, Company C to forty-four.

Since November 16 the 4th Division had fought in the forest; its maximum advance had been just over three miles. Some 432 men were known to be dead; another 255 were missing and probably dead. The division had incurred a total of 4,053 battle casualties, while an estimated 2,000 more men had succumbed to nonbattle causes. That was 2,000 casualties per mile of gain.

Late on the first day of December, "Tubby" Barton talked at length with his corps commander about the condition of his command. Joe Collins promptly authorized Barton to stop all attacks. Two days later, another fresh unit from the relatively inactive Ardennes front, the 83d Infantry Division, would begin to arrive to relieve the 4th.

Still another division was to test the Huertgen Forest.

So long as the Germans held the Brandenberg–Bergstein Ridge, from which German gunners had so unmercifully pounded the Vossenack Ridge during the drive on Schmidt, few could believe that the 8th Division's attack would stop with the taking of Huertgen and Kleinhau. The First Army needed the Brandenberg–Bergstein Ridge to anchor the south flank of the drive to the Roer River. What was more, holding the ridge might provide a bonus, should anybody ever get around to retaking Schmidt and eliminating the Roer River Dams.

The spine of the Brandenberg–Bergstein Ridge was open, but dense forest encroached on the slopes and at a point west of Brandenberg merged across the crest of the ridge at a slight dip in the terrain. Since the 5th Armored's CCR remained attached to the 8th Division, the obvious choice for moving from Huertgen down the spine of the ridge was the armor. But with memory of CCR's premature commitment against Huertgen still vivid, neither the new 8th Division commander, "Wild Bill" Weaver, nor the V Corps commander, Leonard Gerow, was content to see the armor try the job alone. It was finally decided that the 121st Infantry would clear the woods north of the ridgeline as far as the "dip," while the 28th Infantry Regiment was moving from Vossenack to sweep the woods south of the ridge. Only then was the armor to move.

When, on November 30, they began to clear the woods, the infantrymen of both the 28th and the 121st Regiments came upon the familiar forest pattern: stubborn Germans hiding behind minefields, barbed wire, and log emplacements; lethal shellbursts exploding in the trees; enemy soldiers slipping stealthily past their open flanks; their own tanks and tank destroyers giving them little or no support. Not until darkness came on the second day, December 1, was the forest clear as far as the dip.

As a task force of CCR commanded by Lt. Col. William A. Hamberg moved shortly after dawn on December 2 down the highway toward Brandenberg, it seemed from the first that somebody had come up with the same script used in the abortive attempt against Huertgen. No sooner had the lead tanks reached the dip in the ridgeline than one tank hit a mine. Then fire from German tanks and assault guns far away on the Kommerscheidt–Schmidt Ridge began to find the range. In a matter of minutes, Task Force Hamberg lost four tanks.

Seek defilade positions, General Weaver promptly told the tankers, until engineers could clear the minefield. Considering the observation, that could be accomplished only after night fell. In the meantime, Weaver told his infantrymen to get on with the task of clearing the woods beyond the dip.

Through the night of December 2, engineers from CCR probed carefully through the perilous darkness for mines. As daylight came, they had removed more than 250 mines from the dip, a concentrated and intricately patterned collection. Yet even with this impressive number removed, CCR still was destined to lose two more tanks to mines in the dip.

At eight o'clock the morning of December 3, Task Force Hamberg again started down the road toward Brandenberg. Fortunately, the weather smiled, and P-47 Thunderbolts were quick to take advantage of it. The tank crewmen were delighted.

"Keep the buzz boys up," one tank commander radioed as he raced across the dip toward Brandenberg; "they are doing a good job."

Even after reaching the very threshold of the village, the tankers were loath to relinquish their air support.

"Keep the buzz boys up!" the tank commander radioed again; "we are at a critical stage!"

Six minutes later the tanks were inside Brandenberg, cruising the streets, shooting up the landscape. Close behind them in halftracks rolled the armored infantrymen. Spilling from their vehicles, they spread quickly through the village to round up a cowed enemy.

In an hour it was over. Brandenberg was clear.

In the confusion and excitement of the attack, a platoon leader in charge of three tanks, Lt. George Kleinsteiber, roared all the way past Brandenberg half a mile into Bergstein. Quickly knocking out two antitank guns, Kleinsteiber and his companions might have seized the entire village had not Colonel Hamberg called them back. His force, Hamberg believed, was too weak to defend both villages against counterattack.

Chance of quick capture of Bergstein passed with this recall, for no force was immediately available to come to Hamberg's aid. Earlier in the day, General Weaver, with unfortunate timing, had committed the rest of CCR to a subsidiary task of clearing the Germans from a hold-out position among a rubble of houses in the northeastern end of Vossenack.

The armor could expect little help from the infantry, for as always in the forest fighting, the infantry battalions had incurred serious losses, particularly the long-committed 121st Regiment. Here, in sober language, was how a regimental staff officer saw the plight of one unit:

The men of this battalion are physically exhausted. The spirit
and the will to fight are there; the physical ability to continue is
gone. These men have been fighting without rest or sleep for four
days and last night lay unprotected from the weather in an open
field. In some instances men were forced to discard their overcoats
because they lacked the strength to wear them. These men are
shivering with cold, and their hands are so numb that they have to
help one another on with their equipment. I firmly believe every
man up there should be evacuated through medical channels.

Not all the battalions were so bitterly fatigued or so woe-
fully depleted as this one, but all were a far cry from the stalwart formations that first had entered the Huertgen Forest a
fortnight before. So physically and morally fatigued were some
men that they would not stay in the line. Court-martial cases
grew to disturbing proportions. During the night of December
3, a sleet storm coated the trees and fields with a blanket of
ice, to add to the other miseries.

To the hard-pressed Americans, it seemed that their adversary was immune to the rigors of the forest, the shells, and
the weather. In reality, this was untrue, but since the Germans
were almost always on the defensive, they had better cover
from the shelling and the elements. "Great losses . . . from frostbite," one German commander recalled later; "in some cases
soldiers found dead in their foxholes from sheer exhaustion."
And more than once American troops came upon grim, mute,
nauseating testimony to the effectiveness of their own artillery
fires. Paul Boesch's Company G, 121st Infantry, for example,
moving through the darkness to a line of departure to attack
Huertgen, had come upon "a ghastly column" of dead soldiers
and horses. "The stench was overwhelming," Boesch recalled.
"Bloated men and horses, some of which had burst, lay full in
our path. We had to step high to shake the entrails off our
boots." Another company, penetrating the woods north of
Brandenberg, came upon "a mass" of dead Germans, dead
horses, and abandoned vehicles.

At German command levels, the new American thrust toward Brandenberg and Bergstein caused concern. Along the
Roer River farther downstream, German commanders could
note, the Americans would hardly dare jump the Roer until the

dams near Schmidt were in hand; for downstream the land is flat, and waters from the Roer reservoirs would inundate vast acres of ground. Not so near Bergstein. Here the Roer runs in a deep gorge, which American engineers might conquer with high bridges that could withstand even a sudden flood released by blowing the dams. Privy to Hitler's plans for the counter-offensive in the Ardennes, the *Seventh Army's* General Brandenberger searched far and wide for some unit to throw into the fight, lest the counteroffensive—its target date less than two weeks away—be forestalled by a crossing of the Roer.

Though failing to share his concern fully, higher commanders nevertheless thought seriously enough about the threat posed by the 8th Division to take an unusual step. For the first time during the battle of the Huertgen Forest, they released some of the fighter aircraft that had been carefully hoarded for the counteroffensive. During the afternoon of December 3, some sixty Messerschmitt 109's roared in over the V Corps sector. They chose a propitious time to strike, for the P-47's that had helped CCR take Brandenberg that morning already had hurried home as weather closed in at their bases.

Bombing and strafing, the Messerschmitts attacked for more than an hour. To most of the American troops, it was a unique experience, for even the most seasoned rarely had seen more than one or two German planes at a time.

"Send up more .50-caliber ammunition," radioed an officer of CCR from Brandenberg. "We've knocked down three Me. 109's and there are still plenty to shoot at."

It was with much this same spirit that most men of the 8th Division and the V Corps appeared to accept the *Luftwaffe's* strike. Antiaircraft units, which for months had seldom seen a plane to shoot at, were ecstatic over the opportunity. They knocked down nineteen of the aircraft and claimed ten others probably destroyed. As for the effectiveness of the strike, not a man in the V Corps was killed, not a man wounded.

The *Seventh Army* commander, Erich Brandenberger, meanwhile continued to search for a ground unit to forestall loss of Bergstein and regain Brandenberg; for almost nothing remained now of either the 275th or 344th Division or any of the makeshift units that from time to time had been brigaded together under the *275th Division*. At long last, Brandenberger gained permission to use two-thirds of the *272d Volks Grenadier Division*, a unit already defending in the Monschau Corridor and scheduled to fight in the winter counteroffensive. With the authority came the proviso that the *272d* had to be released in time to absorb replacements for the counteroffensive, scheduled now for December 16.

Thus began another of the races against time that had been a feature of so much of the fighting along the German frontier since the *12th Division* had intervened dramatically in the Stolberg Corridor almost three months before. Now the question was whether Brandenberger could move two regiments and artillery support of the *272d Volks Grenadier Division* into Bergstein before General Weaver and his attached armor renewed their attack.

This time the Americans won, but with less than half a day to spare.

Not until the morning of December 5, two days after Brandenberg fell, did CCR's second task force finish clearing the "rubble pile" at Vossenack and become available to help at Bergstein. While tank destroyers provided overhead fire from commanding positions in Brandenberg, the tanks and armored infantry struck in three columns. In a matter of minutes they raced across the half-mile of open ground between the two villages and gained the first houses in Bergstein. There followed a methodical mop-up that ended only after dark, when all the rubble of Bergstein was in hand.

In hand, yes, but cruelly exposed to counterattack should the Germans strike back, for the best efforts of the depleted American infantry battalions still had left great stretches of forest on north, south, and east of Bergstein to the Germans. Also remaining to the Germans was a dominating wooded height at the eastern end of the village, Burg-berg, or Castle Hill. Neither CCR nor the 8th Division had anybody to send to take this hill. The combat command was now down to 400 men, including the crews of six remaining tank destroyers and sixteen tanks, and every man of the 8th Division, including the division engineer battalion, was in a foxhole somewhere.

The counterattacks began before dawn the next morning, December 6. Supported by five tanks, men of the *272d Volks Grenadier Division* used the darkness to gain access to the village. Here the fight raged at close quarters. Only with the coming of daylight was CCR able to bring its superior armor strength to bear. The Germans fell back, but they continued to chew at the village all day long with artillery and assault-gun fire directed from Castle Hill, and twice more they tried to come out of the woods to storm the village.

As night came, the condition of CCR raised grave doubts whether the armor could continue to hold so long as the Germans retained the dominating height of Castle Hill. Tanks in the combat command now numbered only seven, just over a platoon.

To corps commander General Gerow, "Wild Bill" Weaver appealed for help. Gerow in turn gained approval from the First Army's General Hodges to commit a special unit, the 2d Ranger Battalion, to seize Castle Hill the next morning before daylight.

An elite force, specially trained for hazardous missions such as taking a line of cliffs overlooking the invasion beaches in Normandy, the Ranger Battalion in a night attack quickly swept the tree-crowned crest of Castle Hill. Holding it was another matter, particularly in the face of incessant German shelling, most of which burst in the treetops. By the time, two days later, that General Weaver was able to adjust his lines and free an infantry battalion to defend the hill, the Rangers were down to a fourth their original strength.

Obliged to release the men of the *volksgrenadier* division for the counteroffensive, General Brandenberger of the *Seventh Army* now had no choice but to abandon his efforts to retake the ridge. Heterogeneous small units still would make a fight of it as infantry of the 8th Division sought to clear the woods down to the waters of the Roer, but by nightfall on December 8 the worst was over.

"You can say," remarked one officer of the 8th Division, "that we got to the Roer River by sheer guts."

A look at the casualty figures bears him out. During the battle that had begun eighteen days earlier, on November 21, units of the 8th Division and the 5th Armored's CCR had incurred approximately 4,000 casualties. Another 1,200 had succumbed to the elements or to combat fatigue.

Victim Number 5 had fallen to the Huertgen Forest.

AN END TO THE GLOOM, THE MISERY

18 By the end of the first week of December, all three corps of the Ninth U.S. Army had planted their standards on the west bank of the Roer River downstream from Dueren. This they had accomplished after a costly fight across muddy fields and through stanchly defended villages of the Roer Plain. Other than the First Army's V Corps, which had participated in the big offensive only in a supporting role, the one corps still with some distance to go before reaching the Roer was Joe Collins' VII Corps. This, ironically, was the force which as "main effort" had received heavier air and artillery support.

The explanation was, of course, the Huertgen Forest.

It was on December 3 that events made it abundantly clear to both Joe Collins and his superior, Courtney Hodges, that the VII Corps had to have new strength before seeking to conquer the three miles remaining before the Roer River. That was the day when a counterattack in no more than company strength nearly rolled up the 4th Division's feeble 22d Infantry at the woods line near Gey, the same day that two companies of the 1st Division's 26th Infantry perished at Merode.

By the end of the first week of December, the VII Corps presented an altered face for an attack scheduled to begin on December 10. Having fought farther north, fully outside the Huertgen Forest, the 104th Division remained basically intact and stayed in the line. The 3d Armored Division also stayed as corps reserve. In place of the 1st Division came Louis Craig's 9th Division, recuperated after a month's rest from the grim September and October fighting in the forest. Replacing the 4th Division was the 83d Division under Maj. Gen. Robert C. Macon, a unit with long combat experience in Normandy. Because the 83d Division was to continue with the 4th Division's old assignment of driving northeast on Dueren, the entire 5th Armored Division (minus CCR on the Brandenberg–Bergstein Ridge) moved to Kleinhau and Grosshau, whence it was to attack east and southeast to the Roer as soon as the 83d Division had opened roads beyond the last fringe of the Huertgen Forest.

One regiment of the 83d Division still had as much as a mile to go before emerging from the Huertgen Forest. The other two, having replaced the 12th and 22d Regiments near Gey, still had to fight their way out of the forest onto open ground.

The Germans opposite the 83d Division still were part of Erich Straube's *74th Corps,* though the corps was destined on the day the Americans attacked to come under the aegis of General von Zangen's *Fifteenth Army* (alias *Gruppe von Manteuffel.*) This was to permit General Brandenberger and headquarters of the *Seventh Army* to move south for their role in the big counteroffensive. The German division still in control of this sector was Mahlmann's *353d Infantry Division.* Also still around were remnants of the *344th Infantry Division,* which preceded the *353d* into the forest; but these were scheduled for early relief so the division might be rehabilitated for the counteroffensive.

As the big guns on the American side announced another attack early on December 10, thrusts of the 9th and 104th Divisions on the open ground west and northwest of Dueren began to make slow but steady progress. As always, the real problems developed farther south, in the Huertgen Forest.

Because of delays in relief of the 4th Division's 8th Infantry, the 329th Infantry on the 83d Division's north wing was not to begin its drive to pierce the remaining mile of forest until two days later. Thus all eyes—including those of General Mahlmann and his *353d Division*—focused on the other two regiments. These two regiments were to break out of the forest to seize Gey and Strass, the latter less than a mile southeast of Gey. These two villages gather in a number of roads and trails from the Huertgen Forest, subject them to a minor multiplication process, then release them northeast, east, and southeast to the Roer.

Determined to make a strong start, the 83d Division commander, General Macon, assigned a regiment to each village— the 330th Infantry on the right to Strass, the 331st on the left to Gey. Each regiment was to employ one battalion at first. Men from the 331st were to advance astride a dirt road leading from the west into Gey, those from the 330th along an unimproved road meandering from Grosshau through a patch of dense woods past a hamlet called Schafberg to Strass. The outcome of each regiment's attack thus depended in large measure on one muddy, forest-cloaked road, a prospect that might have given considerable pause to veterans of Schmidt, Kommerscheidt, Huertgen, and Merode.

Eager to get into Gey and Strass before daylight provided German infantry perfect fields of fire between the villages and the forest, men of both attacking battalions moved swiftly. On the left, troops of the 331st Infantry picked their way over deeply buried antitank mines and entered Gey shortly before dawn. The battalion of the 330th moved with equal success through the woods toward Schafberg, bypassed that hamlet, and continued to Strass.

In both villages, the Germans fought back tenaciously. To tip the balance between infantry forces of about equal size, the Americans needed tanks, but in mid-morning, when tanks started forward, the trouble began.

On the dirt road west of Gey, three tanks quickly exploded antitank mines. Tracks demolished, they blocked the road. Through this day and the next, engineers tried to clear both this road and the main highway leading from Grosshau to Gey. It was a deadly exercise in futility. Working almost under the eyes of German artillery observers, the engineers took serious losses, and each time they deemed a route cleared, the lead tank would blow up on an undiscovered mine. As the Germans sent reinforcements to Gey, the 331st Infantry commander, Col. Robert H. York, had to send another of his battalions. Without tanks, neither side could gain a real advantage in the village.

First efforts to get tanks to Strass proved more successful. Though an entire company began the trip, one platoon took a wrong turn, blundered into an ambush laid by German anti-tank guns, and was destroyed. The others made it. With their help, the infantrymen in Strass swept the Germans quickly from the village; but back in the woods, the tankers had left nobody to keep the trail open.

That night, December 10, the Germans resorted to an old Huertgen Forest trick of infiltration. In the woods along the dirt road near Schafberg, they emplaced a nest of antitank guns. Into Schafberg, through which the American tanks had passed with no difficulty, they sent a battalion of infantry.

The Americans in Strass were, in effect, cut off.

At daylight the next morning, December 11, a combat command of the 5th Armored Division was scheduled to pass through Schafberg, bypass Strass, then drive southeast to the Roer. Through the night, as reports from supply columns trying to get through to Strass filtered back, the armored division commander, Maj. Gen. Lunsford E. Oliver, expressed increasing concern lest his armor run into trouble at the start.

"The road is about as open as we can get it," General Macon snapped. "We can't keep out the snipers."

But as daybreak neared, accurate reports about the status of the road made it obvious the Germans had holed up at Schafberg in strength. When the 331st Infantry sent a battalion to clear them out, General Oliver sent a battalion of his own armored infantry to help. Yet when night came on the eleventh, the Germans still held Schafberg and effectively blocked the road.

Meanwhile, in Strass, matters went from bad to worse. As daylight came on the eleventh, the Germans counterattacked. All day long they pressed forward under cover of one artillery concentration after another. With the help of their tanks, the

American infantrymen held their own, but the end of the day found the battalion in serious condition. Only seven tanks remained. In two days, the battalion had run through four commanders, two killed, two wounded. Many wounded men needed medical attention badly. All food was gone.

Through all the cost, concern, and frustration of the two days at Gey and Strass, there emerged one bright development. When the 329th Infantry early on the third day, December 12, began to attack through the woods farther north in the direction of Dueren, the German 353d *Division* had already used the bulk of its reserves at the two villages. Though it took the 329th all day to gain the edge of the woods, it was less a question of genuinely stubborn opposition than of the usual travails of the forest fighting—tree bursts, extensive minefields, and the difficulty of maintaining control in the dense woods. The next day, December 13, this regiment was to break out of the forest into a western suburb of Dueren with little enough trouble.

In the meantime, at the two embattled villages of Gey and Strass, the fresh troops of the two regiments of the 83d Division began at last to prevail over the tired German forces. Behind a flail tank borrowed from the 5th Armored Division, a covey of tanks finally reached Gey during the afternoon of the twelfth. Tanks and infantry together set out systematically to clear the Germans from the village. And on the road to Strass, one company after another maneuvered against the settlement of Schafberg. By mid-afternoon of December 12, Schafberg too was clear, but even as the last Germans fell back or surrendered, the road lost much of its critical importance. With the opening of the main highway into Gey, supplies and tanks now might move through Gey, thence down an improved road to Strass.

Hard, serious combat that in some cases would last until Christmas Day, remained for both the 83d Division and the 5th Armored, but the part of their fighting that related directly to the battle of the Huertgen Forest was over. Committed in the forest for only three days, the 83d Division was not punished as severely as were those units that came earlier and stayed longer, yet in three days the fighting still had claimed more than a thousand men. Even the brief commitment of armored infantrymen of the 5th Armored Division in the attack on Schafberg produced 150 casualties.

To the last, the cruel forest demanded a striking toll.

As the fighting in the north moved out of the Huertgen Forest, parts of the forest in the south remained to be cleared. There was, for example, the pillbox strongpoint near the forester's lodge at Raffelsbrand, the position that had defied Lee Chatfield's battalion of the 60th Infantry and, in turn, almost the entire 110th Infantry. There was also some two miles of woods between Raffelsbrand and the Monschau Corridor, not to mention the ruins of Kommerscheidt and Schmidt and the imposing Roer River Dams.

While the 83d Division emerged from the woods at Gey and Strass, the battle of the Huertgen Forest gave every indication of continuing in the south; for at long last, the First U.S. Army was readying an attack aimed specifically at the vital dams near Schmidt. After a few feeble attempts by Allied bombers to destroy the dams from the air, General Hodges finally had faced up to the incontrovertible fact that he had to seize them by ground attack. Thus, as the Ninth U.S. Army, soon to be joined by the VII Corps, waited impotently along the west bank of the Roer downstream from the dams, Hodges told Gerow's V Corps to take the dams.

Back at the end of November, when the 8th Division finally captured the village of Huertgen, one reason Hodges and Gerow had sent that division down the Brandenberg–Bergstein Ridge was to prepare for possible attack south from the ridge across the Kall River gorge to Kommerscheidt and Schmidt. The tentative plan was to squeeze the dams in a vise. The 8th Division was to attack from the north, another division from the south. In the process, those Germans in the pillboxes of the Monschau Corridor might be trapped.

At the end of the first week of December, the plan was no longer logical, for the 8th Division was in no condition to perform its assignment. Gerow decided instead to supplement the attack from south of the dams with a thrust directly up the Monschau Corridor to Schmidt.

The V Corps offensive to capture the dams began on December 13 across the carpet of deep snow that blanketed the entire Eifel. A new division, the 78th, made surprisingly good progress at first in the Monschau Corridor, while the veteran 2d Division, attacking from the south through terrain remarkably similar to that in the Huertgen Forest, after three days of fighting succeeded in piercing a previously unbroken portion of the Siegfried Line. Prospects were bright for swift gains the next morning, December 16.

Two hours before daylight on the sixteenth, German artillery began to pound both 2d and 78th Division positions with a volume and persistence unknown for a long time. It was alarming, ominous. When day broke, the Germans began to counterattack, not in a half-hearted, poorly co-ordinated manner but in strength and with almost desperate determination.

As the day wore on, it became increasingly apparent that the heretofore quiet sector from Monschau all the way south to Luxembourg had erupted with a fury. Both the 2d and 78th Divisions had to turn from the Roer River Dams to fight for their lives.

The battle of the Huertgen Forest at last was over, brought to an end by the German counteroffensive, the Battle of the Bulge.

THE TRAGEDY OF THE
HUERTGEN FOREST

19

IT WAS OVER.

At last, it was over.

Though roughly one-eighth of the region which Americans and Germans knew as the Huertgen Forest had yet to change hands, the part of the fighting that both sides looked on as the battle of the Huertgen Forest was over.

From September 14, when the 9th Division's 47th Infantry moved through the fringe of the forest toward Schevenhuette, until December 13, when the last of the 83d Division and the 5th Armored emerged into the open at Gey and Strass—three miserable, interminable months—Americans and Germans had been locked in a battle in the Huertgen Forest that had involved a long, grim parade of units on both sides.

Five American infantry divisions—the 1st, 4th, 8th, 9th, and 28th—and Combat Command R of the 5th Armored Division fought full-scale engagements in the forest, and the 9th Division, in effect, fought there twice. In addition, the 83d Division and the rest of the 5th Armored got a short, bitter taste of the forest. Numbers of supporting tank, tank-destroyer, cavalry, chemical, medical, and artillery units—some of them sizable forces, like the 1171st Engineer Combat Group, the 4th Cavalry Group, and the 2d Ranger Battalion—also fought in the forest. These units represented a force of approximately

120,000 men, and individual replacements augmented the number by many thousands.

More than 24,000 Americans, killed, missing, captured, and wounded, fell prey to the forest fighting. Another 9,000 succumbed to the misery of the forest itself, the wet, and the cold —trench foot, respiratory diseases, combat fatigue.

The total: 33,000.

This was strikingly high, particularly in terms of the strengths involved and the ground gained. In World War II, losses of 10 per cent were considered high. These were losses of more than 25 per cent.

Six German divisions—the *47th, 89th, 275th, 344th,* and *353d Infantry Divisions* and the *116th Panzer Division*—fought in the forest. Parts of two others—the *12th* and *272d Volks Grenadier Divisions*—also participated. With supporting units, plus special task forces like *Regiment Wegelein,* this probably represented some 80,000 men, again strongly augmented by individual replacements.

Because the Germans lost many of their records, arriving at an accurate accounting of their casualties is difficult. The best estimate is that their losses equaled those of the Americans, which means that the Germans lost a considerably higher proportion of the troops engaged.

In the broad picture, the fighting in the Huertgen Forest was not the only slow, bitter, costly campaigning during the fall of 1944. It was slow, bitter, and costly all along the Western Front as the overextended Allied armies, supply lines taut, came up to the German frontier. Here Allied problems multiplied because of narrowing corridors of advance, inhospitable terrain and poor campaigning weather. The Germans meanwhile gained strength from internal communications and from the Siegfried Line.

Nobody got very far anywhere during the fall of 1944. British and Canadians, with the help of an airborne army, cleared Holland up to the Maas River and opened the port of Antwerp. The Ninth U.S. Army and part of the First reached the Roer River, seventeen miles inside Germany. While the

Third Army drove from the Moselle River to the German border facing the Saar, the Seventh Army and the First French
Army gained most of the west bank of the Rhine along the
upper reaches of the river.

That was all.

The remarkable fact about the entire fall campaign was
that even though the Germans had never held the initiative,
they, more than the Allies, had controlled the outcome. Making
an incredible recovery from the summer defeat in Normandy—
a "Miracle of the West" in answer to World War I's "Miracle of
the Marne"—they gave up ground so grudgingly that the basic
conditions that Hitler as early as September had deemed essential for launching his winter counteroffensive were all met when
the counterblow fell. And through it all they managed to amass
the reserves for the counteroffensive.

All this was as true about the fighting in the Huertgen Forest as it was elsewhere on the Western Front. Here a cagy, im-
perturbable army commander, Erich Brandenberger, guided
by the master of improvisation of *Army Group B*, Field Marshal Walter Model, had hoarded his meager resources and fed
them to the points of real crisis with an almost uncanny sense
of timing. So successful were Model and Brandenberger in
using the forest to advantage for the delaying action they required, despite limitations in manpower, airpower, equipment,
and supply, that little criticism can be directed at the broad
German conduct of the battle.

On the other hand, how successful would Brandenberger—
and even Model—have been had American commanders gone
about the campaign some other way?

No critical analysis of the battle of the Huertgen Forest, or
of the entire campaign around Aachen during the fall of 1944,
can be made without mention of the Roer River Dams. For
whether or not General Hodges, his staff, and his corps commanders recognized it at the time, the battle of the Huertgen
Forest revolved around these dams.

Or should have.

Having fought through the autumn to reach the Roer

River, the First and Ninth U.S. Armies were powerless to cross the river until the dams were either captured or destroyed. Thus the Germans in their counteroffensive enjoyed more than a secure north flank resting on the dams. They enjoyed the knowledge that the Americans were powerless to jump the Roer and strike at the base of the counteroffensive.

Not until February 1945, when the Battle of the Bulge was ended and Allied armies were ready to resume their interrupted drive to the Rhine, could the Allies turn their attention to the Roer Dams, which still stood as tyrannical as ever. Just as had been the case since the day Joe Collins launched his reconnaissance in force five months before, nobody could cross the Roer downstream from the dams to exploit the broad invasion route to the Rhine.

Under General Eisenhower's February plans for driving to the Rhine, Canadians of Field Marshal Montgomery's 21st Army Group were to open the offensive on February 8 far to the north, beyond reach of the threat from the Roer. Delaying their attack to permit Montgomery's thrust to draw off a portion of German reserves, the Ninth Army and the VII Corps of the First Army were to jump the Roer and head for the Rhine on February 12. This, of course, assumed prior elimination of the Roer Dams.

General Gerow's V Corps again drew the assignment of seizing the dams. As a corollary of another attack in progress, two divisions, the 2d and 9th, already were heading toward the dams from the south. Gerow designated a third, the 78th, to repeat the interrupted December attack up the Monschau Corridor to Schmidt. During the afternoon of February 4, a company of the 9th Division grabbed the Urft Dam before the Germans could demolish it. Six days later, before daylight on February 10, men of the 78th Division at last reached the big earthen Schwammenauel Dam, downstream from the Urft.

They were too late.

German engineers had destroyed the penstocks of the dam, releasing no major cascade of water, but rather a gradual flow calculated to produce a long-lasting flood in the valley of the Roer. Even without the waters from the Urft reservoir, the flood was sufficient to tie up the Ninth Army and the VII Corps for eleven days past the scheduled attack date of February 12. In the meantime, the Germans were free to throw all the reserves they had left against Montgomery's troops farther north.

On February 23, when the Americans at last attacked, the Roer still was badly swollen, so that engineers trying to throw tactical bridges across the river had to fight a savage struggle with the rampaging current. But they managed it, and in the process the Americans drew their one advantage from the whole affair of the Roer Dams. Having attacked before the Roer fully subsided, they took the Germans on the east bank by surprise.

Anybody who might still have been inclined to doubt the importance of the dams had only to note that the flood from waters of only one of the two big reservoirs forestalled a crossing of the Roer for thirteen days. Had an American force previously crossed the river, these two weeks would have provided sufficient time for German reserves to defeat it in detail before reinforcements could negotiate the flooded river to help.

Yet, what might have happened had the Americans early in the frontier fighting captured the dams or forced the Germans to demolish them? With the dams intact in American hands, the Germans hardly would have risked sending large numbers of troops west of the Roer, for they would have been liable at any moment to severed supply and reinforcement. Had the Germans been forced to blow up the dams, the Americans would have fought, not against German forces adequately supplied and constantly reinforced by fire brigades committed at just the right point and time, but against a force progressively weakening for lack of supply or reinforcement.

The conclusion is inescapable: had the First Army gone for the Roer Dams early in the fighting, there would have been no battle of the Huertgen Forest.

The American approach—or lack of it—to the problem of the Roer River Dams had its roots in the first days of September, when the First Army, far back in Belgium, turned east toward the German frontier. In the aura of unmitigated optimism

of the day, General Hodges chose to approach the frontier and
the Siegfried Line with all corps abreast. Thus no one of the
three overextended, tired, supply-short corps had the strength
individually to exploit a penetration of the border fortifications.
Gerow's V Corps in the Ardennes–Eifel broke the Siegfried
Line in two places, Collins' VII Corps broke it in the Stolberg
Corridor; but neither could capitalize on it.

There were, of course, two other methods of approaching
the frontier—corps in column (or perhaps in echelon) or two
corps forward and one back. Although this would have made
for greater distances between the First Army and neighboring
units, these distances even with three corps abreast were already so tremendous there was no longer any such thing as a
secure flank. Either of these two methods would have provided
a concentrated force at the point of penetration and a reserve
either for reinforcing the penetration or for thwarting a counterattack against the exposed flanks.

As the First Army did it, the error of dispersion was further
compounded by handicapping the one corps of the three that
was headed toward genuinely advantageous terrain. This was
Corlett's XIX Corps, which lost a division just before the turn
to the east and also bore the brunt of the First Army's gasoline
shortage. Ironically, this was the corps that was headed for the
ground that literally and historically is the true Aachen Gap,
the ground immediately north of Aachen. Assuming the pro-
priety of advancing with three corps abreast, the XIX Corps
should have been the one to lead the way.

The movement of Joe Collins' VII Corps to the frontier in
front of the Stolberg Corridor and the Huertgen Forest fore-
ordained some kind of action in the forest; for the Stolberg
Corridor—no true corridor at all, of course—was so narrow
that the corps had to expand either to left or right, and to the
left was Aachen. Once Collins began to attack with no attention to the Roer Dams, an engagement of some degree of inten-
sity in the Huertgen Forest also became inevitable. When all
on the American side continued to ignore the dams, a real battle became, under the circumstances, inescapable.

There were two ways of avoiding the Huertgen Forest.

One was to concentrate north of Aachen in the true Aachen Gap. But this, assuming no effort against the Roer Dams, would eventually have produced a futile build-up along the Roer similar to that which did develop, and the Germans might well have counterattacked from the forest much as Hodges and Collins feared. The other was to strike south of the dams, much as was planned later for Gerow's V Corps but never implemented.

Attack south of the dams admittedly meant entering rugged terrain, little, if at all, improved over the Huertgen Forest. The area also is farther removed from the Cologne Plain, which the First Army wanted to use for the final push to the Rhine. Yet the V Corps in September had attacked in this general area and had penetrated the Siegfried Line with relative ease, only to have to fall back when Hodges put the emphasis behind Collins' drive near Aachen. Also, this was the sector where the Germans in September had fewer troops than anywhere else on the Western Front, a fact well known to American intelligence. It was the belief that American troops had occupied West Wall pillboxes in this sector that had put the fear of God into Erich Brandenberger the night of September 11. What was more, this was the region where in February 1945, after the bitter lesson of the autumn fighting, Omar Bradley of the 12th Army Group wanted to launch a major thrust to bypass the dams and reach the Rhine.

Had the First Army made a major attack here in September by two corps abreast or by one corps backed up by two others, it could have reached the west bank of the Rhine in ten days.

Assuming the impossibility, for whatever reasons, of a major First Army drive south of the dams through the Eifel, the severe fighting in the Huertgen Forest and the entire Aachen sector might still have been avoided by a timely secondary attack to secure the Roer Dams. This should have been done, even at the expense of temporarily weakening the Aachen sector. It need not have been as comprehensive as the attack, planned by the V Corps for early October, aimed at cutting across a corner of the Eifel to gain the Cologne Plain. It could have been aimed directly at the dams, and unquestionably would have succeeded.

Even as late as November, when the 28th Division made its attack to take Schmidt, it was not too late to reach the dams and forestall much of the severe fighting west of the Roer. The addition of one more division from the south, or at most two, might well have insured the success of the 28th Division's attack and capture or destruction of the dams.

The trouble was, it took the 28th Division's tragic experience to reveal to American commanders the importance of the dams, and even then they delayed the unpleasant job of attacking them. Though the First Army had the strength at hand to attack the dams even in concert with the big November offensive, General Hodges insisted that Allied planes first try to destroy the dams from the air. Top air commanders called the proposal "impractical," but at Hodges' insistence, the Royal Air Force, which specialized in low-level, precision attacks, agreed to try. A siege of poor flying weather frustrated the effort until, on December 7, Hodges at last ordered a ground attack.

So long as the Germans held the Roer Dams, there was bound to be a battle of the Huertgen Forest. Yet even if one accepts or forgives the cardinal sin of ignoring the dams and assumes the inevitability of a fight in the forest, questions still arise about the conduct of the battle itself.

What was wrong was the failure at army and possibly corps levels to appreciate fully the incredible advantage that the forest gave to the defender. Never, even to the last, was sufficient strength assembled to do the job quickly and systematically. With but one division attacking at a time, the Germans could with equanimity borrow from Peter to pay Paul.

What was more, every time a new division entered the forest, the various subsidiary tasks almost always assigned introduced a complexity that should have been avoided. An attack in a forest must be handled simply, like a night attack, or else quick confusion and rapid disintegration of the attacking force is almost inevitable.

Even though the First U.S. Army faced tremendous manpower problems all through the fall of 1944 and seldom possessed a reserve larger than a regiment or a combat command, even this much additional strength, if adroitly committed at the proper time and place, might have altered the outcome of any one of the divisional attacks. Certainly it did on the German side. If not reserves, then quick recognition that a division was exhausted, followed by prompt relief by a fresh force capable of exploiting the gains already made. If the Germans, under the guns and bombs of Allied aircraft, were able to shift their divisions, surely the mobile Americans could have done the same.

The trouble appears on the surface to have been a kind of torpor that enveloped American commanders and their staffs as the exaltation of the pursuit passed and the hard realities of continued bitter fighting followed. Feeding this tendency was the disturbing, almost distressing, practice of some subordinate commanders in the Huertgen fighting to conceal from their superiors the extent of their failures. Through the worst of the 9th Division's October fighting, for example, when battalions were often the size of companies or else were battalions at all only by the grace of inexperienced replacements, regiments throughout reported their combat condition as "excellent." On November 6, after Hatzfeld's battalion of the 112th Infantry had broken and run from the Vossenack Ridge and virtually ceased to exist as a unit, the 28th Division operations officer reported, "The 2d Battalion received very heavy and concentrated artillery fire, withdrew to reorganize and then regained their original position." This was patently false.

While the 8th Division's 121st Infantry was fighting in the woods southwest of Germeter, reports each day to General Hodges told of slow going but in every case emphasized gains. The fact was, the 121st Infantry was getting almost nowhere. During the night that Paul Boesch spent in the shallow trench outside Huertgen, almost twenty-four hours before the village was captured, the word to Hodges was that Huertgen already had fallen, though some mopping up remained. While two companies of the 1st Division's 26th Infantry were cut off in Merode, the word to Hodges was that "contact will be reestablished without too much difficulty tomorrow." Actually the fate of these two companies was as good as sealed.

Was it any wonder, then, that corps and army commanders never committed a reserve at a decisive moment? That regiments and divisions continued to draw impossible assignments long after they had ceased to have the ability to execute them?

As part of the battle of attrition against the German armies fought everywhere during the autumn, the Americans in the Huertgen Forest had inflicted their share of casualties on the enemy, though they took as many in return. They also had gained a few yards of real estate, though they could make no use of it until somebody got around to taking the Roer River Dams. They had failed to prevent any German unit from executing its assignment in the winter counteroffensive, but, on the other hand, five of the American divisions that fought in the Huertgen Forest also performed major roles in defeating the counteroffensive.

As reflected in the fairly rapid collapse of the German armies all along the front following their defeat in the Battle of the Bulge, the Huertgen fighting and the other combat during the autumn had left the German forces brittle. When formal victory came on May 8, 1945, the entire German nation was prostrate, as decisively beaten as any modern state has ever been.

It was over.
The little American Passchendaele was over.
Passchendaele with tree bursts was over.
It is not the death of so many men, nor the wounds and the misery of so many others, that is the real tragedy of the Huertgen Forest. That men must die in war must be accepted, and that some parts of the fighting will be more difficult, more miserable, than others is inevitable. A big push south of the Roer Dams might have been just as costly, might have meant just as much misery, but the fighting would have been in

quest of an objective that mattered—the dams. The real tragedy in battle is when men suffer and die for objectives that are not commensurate with the cost.

Those in the Huertgen Forest fought a misconceived and basically fruitless battle that could have, and should have, been avoided.

This is the real tragedy of the battle of the Huertgen Forest.

A NOTE ON SOURCES

THIS STUDY of the battle of the Huertgen Forest could not have been written without the co-operation of a United States Army with a strong sense of the value of history. The story is based primarily on contemporary Army records housed in the National Archives. None is classified, and all are open to the independent researcher.

The official records include, for each level of command down through the regiment, monthly narrative after-action reports, unit journals (comparable to ships' logs), and comprehensive files of messages, map overlays, and staff section reports. These constitute literally thousands of documents for each division.

The official records were supplemented during the war by accounts of "Combat Interviews" that were conducted soon after an engagement by teams of historians in uniform. Often they include observations by the historians themselves. Depending as they do on the memory of the soldier, the interviews vary greatly in quality, but they are essential to rounding out the rather cold, impersonal story to be found in the official sources. In addition, the author himself conducted a number of interviews with major participants.

The story from the German side is similarly based in large

part on official German records, the originals or microfilm copies of which are also available in the National Archives. Because of wartime circumstances, there are great gaps in the record, particularly at the division level; but the more glaring of these have been covered in postwar manuscripts written by former German officers under auspices of the U.S. Army. These are to be found in the Office of the Chief of Military History, Department of the Army. The most important of the official records are daily war diaries of operations, *Kriegstagebuecher*, maintained by all commands, together with supporting documents in annexes (*Anlagen*). Unfortunately, of the records of units involved in the Huertgen Forest, the only ones to survive the war are those of the headquarters of the *Seventh Army* and of the *81st Corps*.

Little has been written or published on the Huertgen Forest in either German or English. The only published work of value for this study is Paul Boesch, *Road to Huertgen—Forest in Hell* (Houston: Gulf Publishing Company, 1962), a vivid personal account. An unpublished manuscript on the 9th and 28th Divisions has been of particular value: Maj. Henry P. Halsell's "The Huertgen Forest and the Roer River Dams," a copy of which is in the Office of the Chief of Military History.

The author of this volume earlier wrote the official account of the Huertgen Forest fighting for the Office of the Chief of Military History. Fully annotated and considerably more detailed than the present work, this account is soon to be published, as part of a broader account of all First and Ninth Army fighting during the autumn of 1944, under the title *The Siegfried Line Campaign*. The Schmidt story was told in greater detail by the author in the official Army volume, *Three Battles: Arnaville, Altuzzo, and Schmidt* (Washington, 1952).

Incidental direct quotations in the present work are from the following: unit journals and staff section reports; a diary kept by General Hodges' aide-de-camp, Maj. William C. Sylvan; combat interviews; and official German records.

The detailed account of the German private in Chapter 8 is from "The Story of Pfc. Herbert Gripan," found in VII Corps G-2 (intelligence) files for October 1944. That of 1st Lt. Paul

Boesch in Chapter 15 is from Boesch's book, noted above. That of Private Sussman in Chapter 17 is from "The Story of Private Morris Sussman" in 4th Division Combat Interviews; that of the German aid man, from a captured diary owned by Dr. William Boice, of Phoenix, Arizona, formerly chaplain of the 22d Infantry; and that of a regimental staff officer in Chapter 17, from 8th Division Combat Interviews. The brief quote from Ernest Hemingway in Chapter 1, repeated in Chapter 19, is from the novel *Across the River and Into the Trees* (New York: Charles Scribner's Sons, 1950).

In appreciation for its help in making this work possible, the author again acknowledges the United States Army. Fully cognizant that the story of the Huertgen Forest is not a pretty one, the Army has made no effort to suppress it, or, indeed, any other story that does not, in fact, endanger the security of the nation.

My appreciation also goes to those who have given their impressions by interview and by letter, particularly to the former VII Corps commander, General J. Lawton Collins (U.S.A., Retired), a gentleman and a distinguished soldier. I am grateful also for the assistance with records by Mrs. Lois Aldridge and Mr. Rowland Gill; for the assistance with German materials by Mr. Lucian Heichler; for incidental help and encouragement from Mr. Carl Heintze; for the permission of Major Sylvan to use his diary; and for the assistance above and beyond the call of duty by my friend and critic Mr. Martin Blumenson. My sincere appreciation too to my editors, Mr. Hanson Baldwin, Mr. Stewart Richardson, and Mr. Bernhard Kendler.

All interpretations, analyses, and observations are mine alone and are intended in no way to reflect the views of the Department of the Army, the Office of the Chief of Military History, or any individual but myself.

Portree, Washington 22, D.C.

Charles B. MacDonald

INDEX

CPSIA information can be obtained at www.ICGtesting.com
Printed in the USA
BVOW05s1200120614

356170BV00001B/66/P